DATE			

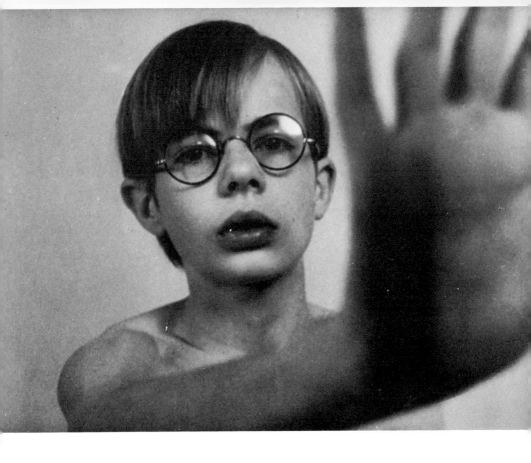

a creation of Halcyon Enterprises

Ingmar Bergman
directs

John Simon *Ivan*, 1925 -

A Harvest Special
H·B·J Harcourt Brace Jovanovich, Inc.
New York

Excerpts from *Winter Light* are from *A Film Trilogy* by Ingmar Bergman. This
translation is copyright © 1967 by Calder & Boyars, and is reprinted by permission
of Grossman Publishers.

Printed in the United States of America

A B C D E F G H I J

Library of Congress Cataloging in Publication Data

Simon, John Ivan, date
    Ingmar Bergman directs.

    (A Harvest special, HB 275)
    "A creation of Halcyon Enterprises."
    1. Bergman, Ingmar, date   I. Title.
[PN1998.A3B4677 1974]   791.43'0233'0924   73-12895
ISBN 0-15-644360-0

CONTENTS

Foreword   9

Conversation with Bergman   11

Bergman Becoming Bergman   41

The Clown's Evening (The Naked Night)   48

Smiles of a Summer Night   106

Winter Light   140

Persona   208

Filmography   313

Acknowledgements

All photographs from *The Clown's Evening:* courtesy Janus Films.
All photographs from *Smiles of a Summer Night:* courtesy Janus Films.
All photographs from *Winter Light:* courtesy Janus Films.
All photographs from *Persona* and photographs on pages 15, 22, 23, and 32, 33, 38: courtesy United Artists Corporation.
Persona: © MCMLXVI A.B. Svensk Filmindustri. All rights reserved.
Photographs on pages 13, 16, 18, 19, 24, 25 and interview quotes on pages 11–40: courtesy Lewis Freedman and The National Broadcasting Laboratory. Quote on page 288: courtesy Lewis Freedman.
Photographs on pages 21, 26, 28, 29, 34: courtesy Janus Films.
We are most especially grateful to William Becker of Janus Films and Lewis Freedman for their co-operation.

FOREWORD

The following study of Ingmar Bergman concentrates on what I consider to be his four most important films to date. Thus it is not a comprehensive account of Bergman's work; it is however a detailed, minute examination of four of its high points, representing different stages and aspects of his genius. Taken together, these four analyses should convey, I hope, the range and nature of his mastery almost as well as a book dealing with each of Bergman's films, but then, of necessity, in less detailed fashion.

For the selection, arrangement, and annotation of the illustrations, all credit should go to Sybil Taylor and Ulrich Ruchti, the editors and technical directors of this series of film books. I wish to thank also, for their most helpful co-operation, Lillian Gerard and Willard Van Dyke of the Museum of Modern Art, William Becker of Janus Films, Margareta Tegnemark of the Swedish Information Center, and, especially, Sharon Mitchell. No thanks, however, to United Artists, who refused to screen Persona *for me.*

—JOHN SIMON

9

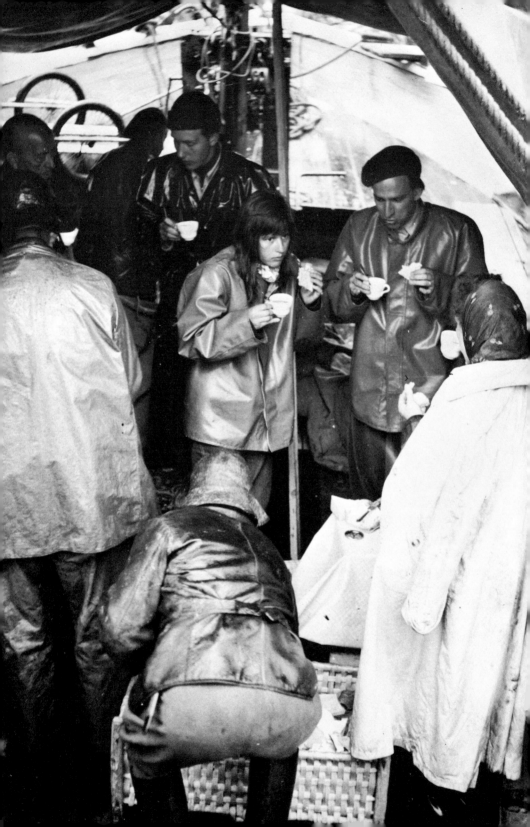

CONVERSATION WITH BERGMAN

B. I am always in a very strange mood when people come to do interviews with me, complicated interviews, because I always have the feeling that I am responsible for some cousin or far-away brother, somebody whom I don't know very well, but am answerable to. Well, when we discuss this person, this Ingmar Bergman, we have to discuss him carefully and I will try to be as open as possible, but I never have the feeling that we are talking about me.

S. It must be a great responsibility, I was thinking, just to be you; because film is probably the most important art today and I think you're the most important film-maker in the world. To be the most important man in the most important art is a terrible responsibility. Does it bother you?

B. No. I never think along those lines. My thinking does not work that way, because when I start writing a new picture, or start shooting or cutting it, or when I release it to the audience, it's always the first time, and always the last time. It's an isolated event, and I never think back or forward; it's just that. Of course, I have amassed a lot of experience over twenty-five or twenty-six years and thirty pictures and, of course, I have a lot of hopes and desires about what I want to do with what is still far away; but my relation

Bergman: "When we begin a film the actors know as little about it as I do." He and the actors embark on a journey.

to my work, my film work and my theatre work, is completely un-neurotic. I'm just a professional; I'm just a man who makes a table or something that is to be used, and the only thing that interests me is that it be used. Whether it is good or bad, a masterpiece or a mess, has nothing to do with the making, with my creative mind. So, my reply is: I feel responsible only for the craftsmanship being good, for the thing having the moral qualities of my mind, and, if possible, for my not telling any lies. Those are my only demands. When I make my pictures, I never place myself in relation to the New Wave or to my other pictures, or to Fellini, or to the cultural situation in the world today, or to television, or anything else. I just make my picture. Because if I started to think this way and that, there would be no picture. So, I have all my difficulties, and get all my joy, just handling the material.

S. Well, then, is it difficult to talk about your old films, is it something you dislike doing?

B. No, it's the past; it's very far away. If it's necessary, we can talk about it; if it's not necessary, better yet.

S. You said a minute ago that you were entering the phase when you were beginning to collect your materials. How long does that phase usually last, and is that a difficult period?

B. No, the collecting is very nice; the dreaming, the playing with the material, surrounding oneself with a lot of notebooks in which to jot down things. That is a marvelous time, a nice creative time.

S. How long do you spend on that?

B. Sometimes a few months, sometimes years. But when I have to sit down to write, to start from the beginning and write the script, that is the hateful period—when I have to make up my mind about what I am going to do and actually write it. I don't like to sit still. I don't feel comfortable when I write, so I have to saddle myself with a lot of discipline day after day.

S. How many hours a day?

B. Four or five. I start at ten o'clock or thereabouts, and I'm free at three. That's just sitting and writing; it takes me about two and a half months; yet I have to do it.

S. But you don't go back to it in the evening, do you?

B. No, never. At three o'clock I have my tea and then I'm free. But of course, when I've been going on for a few weeks, I can't let go of it; it comes back at night or in the early morning. It is a bad, painful time, and I don't like it, but I have to do it. Because I can't just write down ten or twenty pages and go out with a crew and

12

Bergman on the road

improvise. I am no improviser: I must always prepare everything.

S. I don't think that improvisation is such a good thing, really.

B. It just isn't my way of film-making; my way is selective: a mirroring, reflecting. I put a mirror down; then I select, I take out, I put together.

S. Do you enjoy the shooting period?

B. Very much indeed. Sometimes it is quite boring and frustrating, to be sure. But when we shoot, we are together; the actors, the crew, and I—we give and take; we are a very small group and we have all worked together from film to film; we know one another, and know what to do and how to do it. Sitting down with the cutting tape and editing is also very nice.

S. How long on the average does the shooting period last?

B. About fifty shooting days, sometimes fifty-five, but no more than that. I made *A Passion* in exactly forty-five days, but *Shame* took about fifty-five.

S. And the editing?

B. A very long time. I like the editing very much; I sit down and it takes me a lot of time, as much as three or four months.

S. And you work together with your editor?

B. Yes. She is a nice girl, with much patience, who is exactly as pedantic as I am, and she knows everything. I sit down with her and we go at it together. I hate to sit alone, because I am a complete idiot with machines. I am very fascinated by them, but I don't like them.

S. What about cameras? Do you know very much about photography?

B. Yes, I do. And I have learned everything about the laboratory, about mixing, and sound, and lenses, and everything. Because if I didn't, people would have to tell me things, and I'd be in the hands of those experts. And I don't trust experts. I just trust Sven Nykvist. He is a very fine technician, an aficionado.

*Then the film becomes a journey for the characters—
the human journey in interior and / or exterior time.*
(*Left to right*) Shame, The Seventh Seal, The
Magician, Winter Light

S. Do you tell him exactly what you want, or can he guess it?
B. I don't know how we work because we don't talk very much. We
are very fascinated by lighting. We are always studying light. We
are always aware of light.
S. Do you mean natural light?
B. Yes. The light of reality. And the translation of natural light into
artificial light and what we can do with it, that is our science.
S. Do you feel then that there is quite a difference between working
with Hilding Bladh or Gunnar Fischer, your former cinematogra-
phers, and working with Sven Nykvist?
B. Yes, of course. They were marvelous people, real professionals.
But Sven and I have a special relation; I can't explain it. Sometimes we are very, very unhappy together. It's just like an old marriage. We don't talk very much. We never meet privately. But at
the job, I think, we have a marvelous rapport.
S. Something seemed to happen with the photography in your
films. There was a sudden change that came about in *Smiles of a
Summer Night.* Perhaps it was a different film stock that you started
using.
B. No, no.
S. But there was a new sharpness, a definition, a chiaroscuro. The
blacks were very black and the whites very white. I remember, particularly in the dinner scene, an intensity I had never seen in your
films before, and wondered what had happened.
B. Yes. I think it has to do with faces. Because I am always interested in faces. I just want you to sit down and look at the human

It was my parents who wanted me to go into the church.

face. But if there is too much going on in the background, if the face moves too much, if you can't see the eyes, if the lighting is too artistic, the face is lost.

S. I sometimes have the feeling with your films that one of them comes up with one solution to a problem, and the next one with a different solution to the same problem. That's not deliberate, I suppose; it just happens that way?

B. It just happens. There is no orderly progression, no logic, and there are no rigid guidelines. My pictures always come out of tensions, specific situations, changing conditions. It's always like that. And why one picture appeals and another doesn't, I don't know. People who interview me always try to find a pattern. Of course, it's their profession. It isn't mine. My creative life is movement. It's like water. I don't want to be logical or find motives. That is completely uninteresting to me.

S. This is perhaps an unfair question; but does a film begin with some kind of a specific idea: what is it like to go mad, or what is it like to stay together with someone you don't love any more? Is there some kind of simple nucleus around which you build up a film?

B. No. It always starts very secretly; I don't know exactly what is going on. It starts with a sort of tension or a specific scene, some lines, a picture or something, a piece of music. It just starts as a very, very small scene. And from this little scene comes a trembling. I look at it and try to pull it out. And sometimes it remains just this little thing. But sometimes it's more; I can't stop and suddently I have a lot of material. So I never know exactly.

S. When you say "a piece of music," for example, are you listening to a piece of music and it suggests an idea to you?

B. Yes, very often.

S. It becomes a shape somehow?

15

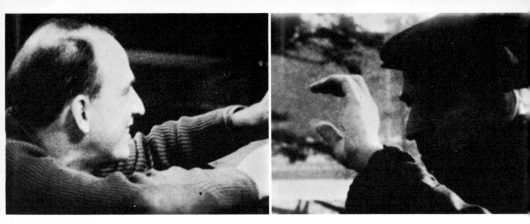

Bergman composes his films: "The whole process is essentially creative. You write down a melodic line and after that, with the orchestra, you work out the instrumentation."

B. Yes.

S. You are very fond of Bach and Mozart?

B. I'm very fond of music. I can't say I have a favorite composer or period.

S. Whom are you interested in now?

B. I think Monteverdi. His is very strange, very modern.

S. Have you ever liked twentieth-century composers?

B. Yes. I'm very fond of music. I like all sorts. I like pop and the Beatles and those protest singers.

S. Do you care for painting?

B. No, not very much.

S. Does this mean that you're not even very interested in it, or just that it doesn't affect your work? You don't like to go to museums, for example?

B. No. Of course, when I come to Amsterdam, I feel it a duty to go to the Rijksmuseum; or when I come to Paris, I go to see the Impressionists. And here we have the Gauguin exhibition and tomorrow I want, if possible, to see it; but it is not necessary.

S. But music is necessary?

B. Yes, music is absolutely necessary. It is the same thing with poetry. Poetry is not necessary, but books are.

S. What kinds of books?

B. All of them. Don't you think that when you are young, you read a lot of books? I have a good example: I like Strindberg very much and he has written a lot of plays but also a lot of prose: novels and short stories, and when I was young I read them all—I had the feeling I had read them. This summer, because of directing *A Dream Play,* I started to read a Strindberg novel and suddenly I realized, yes, I read it when I was twenty-two, but I had not understood it, so I started to reread everything that Strindberg has written, except his plays. It was a fascinating experience. I like enormous books, enormous novels, the Russians.

S. Has Strindberg the dramatist been a great influence on you?

B. Yes. I have been reading him since I was twelve or thirteen, and he has followed me around all my life.

S. How about Proust?

B. Yes, I'm just going on with Swann in *A la Recherche du temps perdu.*

S. What about Joyce, which must be very difficult, I imagine?

B. Yes, that is too much for me. I have read *Ulysses* but it was out of duty more than anything else.

S. Was it the language that made it so difficult?

B. I read it in a Swedish translation because I read extremely slowly.

S. Even in Swedish?

B. Yes, when I read, I read as slowly as if I were reading aloud. It takes me a lot of time, but I remember everything. I don't know why the slowness, but perhaps it's my profession: when I read a play I read as if it were being acted.

S. In connection with *Hour of the Wolf* and *The Magician,* I noticed a certain indebtedness to E. T. A. Hoffmann. He must be someone you like.

B. Yes, very much.

S. Was he relevant to *The Magician?*

B. More to the *Hour of the Wolf.* In *Hour of the Wolf* I really played with him.

S. Do you have any absolute favorites among your films?

B. No. They are old pictures and already far, far away.

S. Do you always like the latest one best?

B. No, on the contrary; the latest one is like an infant: it protests and it makes difficulties and it is very much alive. Sometimes I like it and sometimes I dislike it, but in a very unneurotic way. No, I think I have made just one picture that I really like, and that is *Winter Light (The Communicants).* That is my only picture about which I feel that I have started here and ended there and that everything along the way has obeyed me. Everything is exactly as I wanted to have it, in every second of this picture. I couldn't make

this picture today; it's impossible; but I saw it a few weeks ago together with a friend and I was very satisfied. I very much prefer it to, say, *Through a Glass Darkly,* which, socially speaking, I don't like any more. It's an étude, a study, an exercise; it's a beginning, but it's a pudding. It's so far away, I can't be sure, but my feeling is that it's a pudding, a muddle. Some parts of it are no good, some are really cinematographic, but it can't compare with *The Communicants.*

S. One has the feeling that the Ingmar Bergman figure in the films, at least in the chamber-film phase, is usually Max von Sydow.

B. No, no, not at all. I say, like Flaubert, *"Madame Bovary, c'est moi."* I am all of them, I am inside all of them. It's not especially Max von Sydow or Gunnar Björnstrand or Ingrid Thulin.

S. Do you, when you write a part, have a specific actor in mind?

B. Always, always, yes. It's very important. I always want to know the actor before I write a script. I don't know why, but I hear a voice, and see the behavior. Perhaps it is wrong, I don't know, but we have always worked together.

S. It's wonderful to have such good actors as you have.

B. I think it is good, this tradition here in Sweden, that all are working in the theatre, that we work together in different media.

S. It is interesting to me that some people do not come back in your films, even though I like them. For instance, I like Maud Hansson very much, but I only saw her twice in your films; Margit Carlquist only once. Is there some special reason why they don't reappear?

B. Very neurotic girls. I don't like to work with neurotic people; because they have to *play* neurotics, they should not *be* neurotics; but when they are, they are a disturbance to the work. Because the work in itself is so difficult, we must be very calm and very controlled. The work must be nice, like a family, like joy. We must

have a feeling of security and loyalty. If people are without contact and completely imprisoned in themselves, I can still use them, but they endanger the whole production and I don't like that.

S. The men presumably are less of a problem, because they seem to last longer than the women.

B. Yes. We have grown up together and we have worked together.

S. I wish I could see that documentary that you did about your island, except that I might not understand any of it.

B. It's difficult to understand. It was necessary to make it, to try; you know I've lived there four years now and I know these people and I know their difficulties and I wanted to tell about them and let themselves tell about it all.

S. Was it fun handling the camera yourself?

B. Yet, it's always so; Sven was with me, but I conducted the interviews for the first time in my life. It was a nice experience.

S. Tell me, are there any film-makers that influenced you in any way, that you learned something from, or do you feel completely self-made?

B. No, no, no, no. I have grown up in a tradition. I don't think somebody just becomes a director, you know. We are like stones in a building, all of us. We all depend on the people coming before; I am just a part of this. So, I depend very much on a Swedish film tradition, Sjöstrom and Stiller, and on the Swedish theatre tradition— Sjöberg has meant a lot to me. He is my neighbor. He is marvelous.

Bergman: "I'm actually unable to begin writing until I've made up my mind which actor is going to play the part. Then I suddenly see the actor masked in the part. The part takes on his skin, his muscles, the intonation of his voice, and above all his rhythm, the way he is."
Bergman and Gunnar Björnstrand

And then, you know, when I was young, nineteen or twenty years old, I saw the French pictures—*Quai des Brumes* (*Port of Shadows*), Duvivier and Marcel Carné.

S. Did you like *Les Enfants du Paradis*?

B. Not very much. It's a bit boring. Of course, I liked parts of it. But most of all I liked *Quai des Brumes*.

S. What about *La Règle du Jeu* (*The Rules of the Game*)?

B. They told me that *Smiles of a Summer Night* had some similarities; but I didn't know that, because I hadn't seen it. And then, you know, I have a collection of sixteen-millimeter films, and now I own it.

S. Do you like it?

B. Not very much. I don't like Renoir very much. But then, of course, I always have seen pictures; I like to go to the movies. I'm a moviegoer.

S. What about Carl Dreyer?

B. Yes, in a protesting way.

S. Against it?

B. Yes, some of his pictures have infected me. But in a very strange way, he has always been an amateur. Like Antonioni.

S. I think in a way, you have done what Dreyer wanted to do.

B. Yes.

20

S. But what about Antonioni?

B. I have met him once.

S. Did you get along with him?

B. Yes, we had a wonderful contact. I liked him extremely much. I liked his courage; he is a completely honest man.

S. Whereas Fellini, I think, is not so honest a man.

B. No, no, please! Fellini is Fellini. He is not honest, he is not dishonest, he is just Fellini. And he is not responsible. You cannot put moralistic points of view on Fellini; it is impossible. He is just—I love him.

S. Yes, he is very charming.

B. No, much more than that. I think he has not made his real pictures yet.

S. I think he has made two great films, *The White Sheik* and *I Vitelloni.*

B. Yes, but you know, I am hopelessly in love with this man. Completely. Because, I don't know why, I have met him a few times and . . .

S. This joint project of yours with him has been abandoned, hasn't it?

B. It collapsed. Of course it collapsed, because I am a pedant and he is not.

S. I understand he submitted an outline that was half a page long.

B. Yes, yes, exactly, and I was sitting writing my screenplay.

S. How was it to be? How were the two parts to connect?

B. That was the wrong way from the beginning. That is the damnation of this movie business, in the economical sense. Because, you know, our idea was to choose five or six actors, to have a crew of about six to ten people; to have some money; to have an empty studio and to start and just to make a dialogue and just to invent things, to improvise, to play together.

S. So there was not to be one Bergman half and one Fellini half?

B. No. And then the economic interests came in and the Americans came in, and we tried to explain what we wanted to do. And they said yes, yes, yes—more or less—but then he had no money and he was in a bad situation and he was tired.

S. Fellini?

B. Yes, after *Satyricon,* of course. And he was at work on *Satyricon* and I couldn't wait. Then suddenly we said, all right, I make my part and you make your part, and then we meet in the beginning and at the end. The whole project collapsed at that moment and I

Bergman composes in terms of rhythm. Max von Sydow: "He gives you the distance to the other actor, to the other character. He gives you the rhythm in the action. He gives you the pauses, the increasing speed of the action. He gives you the point where the explosion comes, or where it should have come but it doesn't." (Hour of the Wolf)

am sorry for that. I can teach him something, and he can teach me something.

S. Maybe in the future.

B. Perhaps. When we are older and cleverer. I think it all collapsed because the Americans couldn't understand what we really intended to do. But, really, he was extremely difficult, though that means nothing because I love his work and I love him as a person, if he is a person, which I doubt, because he has no limits; he's just like quicksilver—all over the place. I have never seen anybody like that before.

He is enormously intuitive. He is intuitive; he is creative; he is an enormous force. He is burning inside with such heat. Collapsing. Do you understand what I mean? The heat from his creative mind, it melts him. He suffers from it; he suffers physically from it. One day when he can manage this heat and can set it free, I think he will make pictures you have never seen in your life. He is rich. As every real artist, he will go back to his sources one day. He will find his way back.

S. What I particularly admire in you is that you always change and develop; and as you learn new things you teach them to the world. Very few artists have been able to do that. Stravinsky, Picasso, a few others. But most of them repeat themselves.

B. It's my way of living. I am always curious. It has to do only with

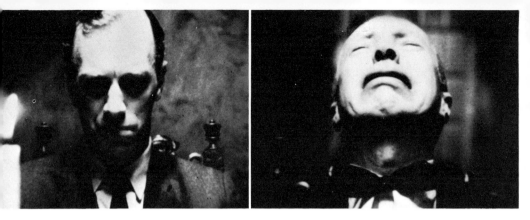

that. No matter how depressed I am, I always wake up in the morning, in the very early morning, a bit curious: what will happen today? Sometimes I am very afraid. But always, always, even if it is completely black—inside and outside—I always feel something very strange—a curiosity.

And then, to express, to be in touch with other human beings. To mix experiences, to be involved; that's my life. If I am isolated or feel no contact or something like that, it is catastrophic for me. So I always try to be in contact. It is very difficult to tell you, but if you have a completely unneurotic relationship—I don't say I'm un-neurotic, because I'm very neurotic—but if you have a non-neurotic relation to your work, it gives you so much joy and helps you such a lot and gives you a form, a discipline, such honest help. So, I just go on.

S. I am only interested in this from your own point of view. Tell me more about your feelings about Antonioni, because I think it'll tell more about you in a way.

B. The strange thing is that I admire him more now that I have met him than when I only saw his pictures; because I have suddenly understood what he is doing. I understand that everything in his mind, in his point of view, in his personal behavior is against his film-making. And still he makes his pictures.

S. How do you mean "against"?

B. It all presents obstacles.

S. What is your favorite Antonioni film?

B. I like most of all *La Notte,* because he had a marvelous actress in it.

S. Yes, Jeanne Moreau. But he didn't do very much with her.

B. No, he never does, he never comes in contact with actors. They don't know what he wants, and he doesn't know how to talk to them.

Yet while actors and director work in and on a common rhythm, they work from different viewpoints. Liv Ullmann: "I was so sorry I was supposed to be in this scene and look at all the heads falling off [chickens being killed]. And I really cried and went away and I heard them laughing. And I didn't understand how they could laugh. But now I see it's the action. For them [director, camera crew] another thing is happening."
(*Shooting* Shame)

S. He knew how to talk to Monica Vitti.

B. I don't think so. But, you know, I like people who even if everything else is against them, continue, and I like and admire . . . I think it was marvelous that this man, this sleepless, tortured, scared man went to America to make a picture about Americans. This is a Don Quixote. And I said to him I could never have courage like that, because I haven't even been in America yet. I think even the thought of going to America, even with a return ticket in my hand, scares me, and I think he had such courage to go to America—to disappear into the desert with his crew and to stay there. He is a strange man, he is a marvelous man, and I admire him very, very much.

S. Perhaps you like the man better than his films.

B. Yes, in a way. Because to me his films always have been a little, little bit boring, and we must be aware that the boring in art is very good in a way, but his is a little bit too boring. But after meeting him, all my reservations are gone.

S. When I first saw *L'Avventura,* I was a little bit bored, too, but on each reseeing it gets bigger and better. Have you seen it more than once?

B. Yes, I like it very much, too. But to go on about directors or film-makers who have influenced me . . . technically, Cukor, very much.

S. In what way technically?

B. In the editing. In the beginning we had no schools here for film-

24

making. The only way of learning film-making was to be an assistant to a director—I was an assistant to Sjöberg—and to see pictures. And we had no film library, we had nothing like that when I was learning. Young students didn't get any money to go abroad; we were shut off, we were just sitting here.

S. How about Hitchcock? Is he someone you learned from?

B. Yes, of course.

S. Technically, I suppose. But isn't there a great intellectual emptiness in his work?

B. Completely, but I think he's a very good technician. And he has something in *Psycho,* he had some moments. *Psycho* is one of his most interesting pictures because he had to make the picture very fast, with very primitive means. He had little money, and this picture tells very much about him. Not very good things. He is completely infantile, and I would like to know more—no, I don't want to know—about his behavior with, or, rather, against women. But this picture is very interesting. I learned a lot from all those Americans who knew their profession.

S. I find it's a terrible notion in modern film criticism that these people were artists, when they were really technicians. We must distinguish between an artist and a technician.

B. Yes, that's important.

S. Modern film criticism tends not to distinguish. People like Raoul Walsh or Howard Hawks don't know what art is. They merely have marvelous techniques, some of them.

B. They have told their stories and they made their films in a good, effective way. That is a duty: effectiveness in telling a story.

S. Yes, that's a very good minimum, but it's only a minimum.

B. But it's difficult.

S. Are there any young film-makers that you particularly like? I hope you don't like Godard?

25

Bergman: "I feel very strongly about the exposed situation of the actors in the face of the outside world. . . . They've got to strip themselves right down to the bare bones. We're always protected. We can make a face or escape through a verbal maneuver. They can't sneak away or explain anything away. They're standing there with their faces and bodies terribly exposed."

Bergman: "You can't make a film without literally directing it. How we achieve direction is a problem worked out in common, by talking and discussing and by fresh suggestions from various points of view. But self-direction I must have, because I am the only one who, at a given moment, pretty well knows how the film is conceived."
(Shooting Wild Strawberries)

B. No, no, no.
S. I detest him.
B. Yes, I do, too. In this profession, I always admire people who are going on, who have a sort of idea and, however crazy it is, are putting it through; they are putting people and things together, and they make something. I always admire this. But I can't see his pictures. I sit for perhaps twenty-five or thirty or fifty minutes and then I have to leave, because his pictures make me so nervous. I have the feeling the whole time that he wants to tell me things, but I don't understand what it is, and sometimes I have the feeling that he's bluffing, double-crossing me. But what about this young Czechoslovakian director, Miloš Forman? Have you seen his work? I like him very, very much.
S. There are other Czechs whom I like better. I think Menzel may be more interesting.

B. Perhaps more interesting, but not to me. No, because Forman has an approach to human beings.

S. There's something a little primitive about him.

B. Yes, I like that very much.

S. What about Bellocchio? Have you seen *China Is Near?*

B. Terrible, *terrible,* very homosexual, very artificial, aggressive in a very empty way.

S. What about the early Truffaut? Did you like those first ones?

B. Very much; very, very much.

S. What's happened to this man?

B. He wants to make money; it's a very human desire. He wants a comfortable life. He wants to make money and he wants people to see his pictures.

S. Well, don't you think his early films were seen by people?

B. But perhaps not by enough, and he didn't make enough money, and he likes the comfortable life of the modern film-maker.

S. But the trouble is his new films are not going to make much money.

B. Then he made a mistake. Because if you lose both the money and your dignity, then it must be a mistake.

S. What about Bresson? How do you feel about him?

B. Oh, *Mouchette!* I loved it, I loved it! But *Balthazar* was so boring, I slept through it.

S. I liked *Les Dames du Bois de Boulogne* and *A Man Escaped,* but I would say *The Diary of a Country Priest* is the best one.

B. I have seen it four or five times and could see it again . . . and *Mouchette* . . . really . . .

S. That film doesn't do anything for me.

B. No? You see, now I'll tell you something about *Mouchette.* It starts with a friend who sees the girl sitting and crying, and Mouchette says to the camera, how shall people go on living without me, that's all. Then you see the main titles. The whole picture is about that. She's a saint and she takes everything upon herself, inside her, everything that happens around her. That makes such an enormous difference, that such people live among us. I don't believe in another life, but I do think that some people are more holy than others and make life a little bit easier to endure, more bearable. And she is one, a very, very simple one, and when she has assumed the difficulties of other human beings, she drowns herself in a stream. That is my feeling, but this *Balthazar,* I didn't understand a word of it, it was so completely boring.

In Bergman's films, various points of view often confront each other within the context of the human condition. Many times, he expresses this concern in his method of identifying the viewer first with one character, then with another. (The Seventh Seal)

S. You could almost say the same thing about the donkey, that when the donkey has taken on other people's suffering . . .

B. A donkey, to me, is completely uninteresting, but a human being is always interesting.

S. Do you like animals in general?

B. No, not very much. I have a completely natural aversion for them. Have you seen this picture *Il Porcile (Pigpen)?*

S. Yes, terrible. I think Pasolini is awful altogether.

B. Yes, awful, awful. Meaningless. Completely.

S. There was a period in your life and work when the question of God was all-important, but not any more, surely?

B. No, it's past. Things are difficult enough without God. They were much more difficult when I had to put God into it. But now it's finished, definitely, and I'm happy about it.

S. In an interview, discussing *Hour of the Wolf,* you said that you believed in demons; but how can you not believe in God, yet believe in demons? Aren't the two things connected? Can one have the one without the other?

B. Well, if I say I believe in demons, of course, it is just a little joke. You sort of want to name things. . . .

S. Things that bother you?

B. Yes, of course. Yet it's not exactly a joke, because when I was younger, not very much younger, say, five, six, ten years ago, and back into my childhood, I was haunted by extremely terrible dreams, sometimes daydreams; sometimes things happened to

me in a very, very strange, mysterious, and dangerous way, and I was very scared, and sometimes my dreams were so real that when I tried to remember something, I didn't know exactly if it had happened in reality or if I had dreamed it. It was very painful; but now it has disappeared—all of those things.

S. Why do you think it went away?

B. I grew up. I worked a lot; I was director of the Royal Dramatic Theatre for three years. I started in the morning at eight o'clock and was there until eleven at night; then I went home and slept. I was at it ten months a year and there was no place left for demons and dreams. Then I went to my island; I have lived there four years. On the island, reality is so real, it's no place for demons and bad dreams. Instead of bad dreams, I now have very ridiculous ones, comical dreams—I often laugh.

S. Can you use those dreams in your work?

B. Perhaps, I don't know. It doesn't interest me any more. To me reality is very real now, and other human beings.

S. More important than dreams?

B. Yes, exactly, and if you have difficulty with your relationships with other people and reality around you, it is a place for demons; but if you are in contact with yourself and other people and reality, there's no room for dreams.

S. Would you say there is a central theme now in your work? Robert Graves, the poet, says that the two real themes, the only themes, are love and death. Do you have any such principal themes?

B. Yes and no. I want very much to tell, to talk about, the wholeness inside every human being. It's a strange thing that every human being has a sort of dignity or wholeness in him, and out of that develops relationships to other human beings, tensions, misunderstandings, tenderness, coming in contact, touching and being

*Viewpoint expresses identity. Bergman films question
identity. What is the common human identity; the
individual identity? How do people relate to one
another, to God, to themselves? He visually unites
characters to express complementary viewpoints
within one identity.* (Persona)

touched, the cutting off of contact and what happens then. That's
what is fascinating. I feel that I have come out into an enormous
field, and I can now get started. I'm very curious about the pic-
tures waiting for me around the corner. It's very difficult to explain.
Because of that I made *A Passion* and my documentary, and be-
cause of that I am writing my new picture (*The Touch*).
S. Then your main theme is interpersonal relations?
B. Yes, but much more so now than before, because I feel much
freer.
S. Is it unfair of me to ask about certain episodes in your films that
I find difficult to understand?
B. No. I will try to be honest.
S. For example, in *Hour of the Wolf,* the episode with the child,
the fishing and the drowning. What is the relationship of the hero
to that boy—is that his son?
B. No, I don't know exactly. I think it was based on a dream I had.
S. You were saying that in *Persona,* those little scenes between
the titles meant the impatience of the film to begin. And you were
talking about your sickness, your ear infection—what was it called
again?
B. Morbus Ménièris; sounds like a dish.
S. It made you lose your balance. How did that affect *Persona?*
B. I was at the hospital for two months, and I wanted to make a
poem of the atmosphere in which *Persona* grew.

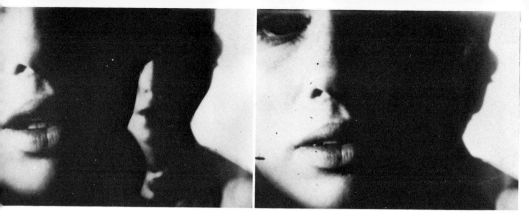

S. Is that why Elisabet is in the hospital for quite a while?

B. No, that has nothing to do with it.

S. Those first shots, then, before the titles, that is the poetry?

B. That is the poetry, yes.

S. And you had that from the beginning?

B. Yes.

S. You began with that? I thought perhaps it was an afterthought.

B. No, but perhaps I elaborated.

S. Is there much change between your script and what happens when you start shooting from it, or do you stay fairly close to it? Some little changes?

B. Yes, in *A Passion* many, because *A Passion* was written in a very strange way; I just dashed it off—not my usual way of writing. Then, I think, I translated it back when I shot it.

S. I find the most difficult part about most of your films is the ending, because the ending always to me is more of a question than an answer. But I'm sure that's what you want it to be. For example, in *Persona* the thing I find very difficult to comprehend is why we only see Alma getting on that bus and why we don't see Elisabet any more. A lot of people have taken this to mean that the whole thing takes place in Alma's mind.

B. It does not. You see Elisabet for a very, very short moment. She's in the studio. She's at work.

S. But it's the same shot you've used before.

B. Yes.

S. So one doesn't know whether that's the future or the past.

B. She's going on. You know here, in the theatre, we play the same play every night for years. So she's back.

S. She's speaking again.

B. Yes.

S. Because that one word which she says, "nothing," that, I think,

Dream and reality are parts of identity. Often they seem interchangeable. Bergman: "The horrifying— the real—drama is always when you dream it very, very realistic. It's only just a small turning of the screw . . . into a reality. Suddenly something happens." (Hour of the Wolf)

she says in one of Alma's dreams. So that's not really Elisabet speaking.

B. Elisabet has come back. She has invented a new aspect of her emptiness and she has filled up with Alma, she has fed on Alma a little bit. And she can go on.

S. Where does that leave Alma? Is Alma eaten up completely?

B. No. She has just provided some blood and meat, some good steak. Then she can go on.

S. And there's enough left for Alma.

B. Yes, Alma is still alive. You must know, Elisabet is intelligent, she's sensible, she has emotions, she is immoral, she is a gifted woman, but she's a monster, because she has an emptiness in her.

S. Do you think most artists have this emptiness?

B. No, it has nothing to do with artists; it has just to do with human beings.

S. So she does not represent the artist?

B. For heaven's sake, no. It was just a way of putting it—it was convenient.

S. But surely a character like the Magician does represent the artist in some way.

B. He is an artist.

S. And Vergérus is the scientist. Was the point there that somehow both of them are struggling for an answer, a different answer, that neither of them can finally come up with—or does somebody

come up with an answer?

B. I have no answers; I just pose questions. I'm not very gifted at giving answers.

S. Was the ending of *The Magician* based on Brecht's *Threepenny Opera* somehow, because of the happy ending out of nowhere?

B. No. It just happened. It was the right way of doing it. I just had the feeling that I had to end with some tour de force.

S. What about something like the last image of *The Seventh Seal,* the Dance of Death? Was that meant at that time to suggest that there is some kind of life after death? I mean was that a form of life, death leading these people, or was that a form of non-existence?

B. When I made *The Seventh Seal,* I was still involved in all these complications. I can't remember exactly.

S. It was a very ambiguous image; it could mean that something goes on after death.

B. Yes, *The Seventh Seal* is, in a way, very concrete, like a medieval play. Everything is there, you can touch everything. The Virgin Mary is real, with the child. When they are dancing, they are concrete; they are. It is not fantasies or dreams or imaginations. It is always my intention to be exact, to be precise, to be concrete; and sometimes I succeed, sometimes not. But my intention is always to be very simple.

S. That was a very concrete image, visually; but what it meant metaphysically was not quite so clear.

B. To me that is not so interesting.

S. Well, then, would you say that *Persona* is really about how a person who feels empty, depleted, and sick gets back into life again by using another person?

B. I don't want to say anything about that. *Persona* is a tension, a situation, something that has happened and passed, and beyond

Place is important. Bergman uses place as an intrinsic, active element in his films. (Shooting Through a Glass Darkly)

that I don't know.

S. Speaking of tensions—does living on an isolated island minimize them?

B. When I write, you know, people say, "Come, come and have dinner with me tomorrow." I say, "No, I can't, because the airplane is booked; it is too complicated to come." So that is that.

S. It's a very practical solution.

B. And when my girl friend and I quarrel and she wants to go away and she is all packed, everything is always too complicated; first she has to drive by a very complicated way through the woods; then, the ferryboat leaves only on the hour; from there, she has to find a flight. So, she ends up staying.

S. At one point it was announced that you would make a film out of

Peer Gynt. Are you still working on that?

B. No.

S. What happened there?

B. Nothing.

S. Then it was not true?

B. Yes. They asked me if I wanted to make a film of *Peer Gynt* after I had done it on the stage.

S. Yes, in Malmö.

B. Yes. I said that could be nice. And they asked how much it would cost, and I said, "A lot of money." "How much?" "Give me five million dollars." Silence!!

S. That's too bad, for we have never seen a good production of *Peer Gynt* in America and your film would have explained what the play is all about.

B. I think the only way to explain the play is to play it on the stage, because a film must be an adaptation; it is not the same thing; you must translate. It's hard work; I prefer to write my own scripts; not adapt; it is too much of a job.

S. My editors, looking at your films on the Movieola, felt that you were fascinated by certain objects, like doors or windows or curtains; do you share that feeling?

B. Yes, it's a bit childish. To a child, a window is very interesting; or a door, or a mirror. My attitudes can sometimes be a little bit childish. Infantile. But if an artist loses his joy in playing, I think he is no artist any longer.

S. Yes, you know Nietszche, who spoke about the child in man?

B. But look at Picasso or Stravinsky. Look at their faces. They are children, grown-up, old, wise children, with wonderful childish eyes. Marvelous!

S. In other words, you find no special symbolic significance in doors? You just like doors.

B. It's fascinating. A door separates you from other people, or you can open it and come in.

S. A mirror probably does have more significance than that. Since you are so interested in faces, a mirror tells you more about a face.

B. Look at a woman. Look at a woman looking in a mirror. It is interesting. Especially if she doesn't see you, if she doesn't know that you see her.

S. What about growing old? Do you have any feelings about growing old in general? Is that a terrible thing?

B. No, no. It's nice. I've got everything; really. I have everything in

*The environment in which his journeys take place
are part of the journey. Bergman (shooting* Shame):
*"You can't imagine what an enormous protest the
sea gives you. You have to put all of your energy,
all of your will, all of your fury to resist saying 'We
go home to the studio and make it with rear
projection.'"*
Interviewer: *"So the fight to make the film, to fight the
ocean, is parallel and maybe part of the tremendous
conflict inside the film?"*
Bergman: *"Yes, yes."*
Interviewer: *"If you did it in the studio tank with rear
projections, the film, the scene itself, would be less
exciting?"*
Bergman: *"Yes, I think it would be a flop, absolutely
catastrophic."*
Liv Ullmann: *"Feeling a bit seasick, being a bit cold,
feeling no good helps us to show how a person is
when he is feeling hopeless."*

life that a man can ask for and I am still curious and I am still looking forward to the film around the corner. The only thing that
troubles me is that I must use eyeglasses.
S. Why does that disturb you?
B. I always forget them and that makes for complications. But
physically I have no difficulties. I feel well. No, growing old doesn't
scare me at all.
S. Isn't it infuriating to think that scientists may discover processes
by which they can freeze people and bring them back to life, and
that we will have lived just a little too early for this?
B. To me it would be no privilege; to me it would be terrible.

S. Why?

B. If you live on an island, at the seaside, with farmers and fishermen, everything has its proportions. Here in the town nothing has proportions. If I am in a bad mood here at the theatre, at a rehearsal, everything grates on my bad mood. Brpphhh. Here in town everything is a little bit perverted. And your reactions seem extremely important to yourself and the contretemps of a spotlight not coming up on this place but on that is an absolute catastrophe. On the island, everything has its proportions; you are a very small part of this island and of the life there. If you scream, it has no effect, nobody hears; or perhaps a bird will fly up. You can make as much noise as you want, you can suffer, and it's only a part of the whole. And it gives to a hysterical mind such as mine—I was born hysterical; it's inherited from my parents—the proportions, the definite proportions of reality, it gives you peace. Because you know you cannot alter anything. That is good and healthy. . . .

S. Let's put it another way. You were talking about your interest in the picture that's still waiting for you around the corner. Suppose you have to die when you are, let's say, seventy-five or eighty, and there's a picture waiting for you around the corner at eighty, which you can never get to. Isn't that a pity?

B. No, it's all right.

S. You think the others are enough?

B. Yes; some people think they are more than enough.

S. Do you feel that your film-making has profited from your work in the theatre, or are they two separate things?

B. Sometimes it's the same and sometimes it's quite different. I have done very much in the studio and in the theatre, and I got good experience from both.

S. What about film actors? Do you think they profit a lot from acting on the stage or can one be a good movie actor without knowing anything about the theatre?

B. Yes, I think you can be a good movie actor without being a good actor on the stage. It is a special talent, being a good movie actor, but I don't know exactly what it is. I think it is a sort of presence, a very strange, creative mind and a very special form of concentration that makes a good movie actor.

S. I must confess I have seldom if ever discovered minds in actors, at least as I conceive of the mind.

B. That's not my experience. They have another way of expressing themselves than we have, and I understand their way very well because I often have the same way of expressing myself. Not when I talk with you but, I tell you, I always think when I talk and if I don't talk, I am intuitive, I have my radar. But when I have to talk and to explain things, I think that I think. I am most of all intuitive and I have trained my intuition; I trust it and always use it in my profession, but I don't discuss with it. So my intuition is my best weapon and my best tool.

S. There is one statement of yours that everybody is always quoting: about your thinking of yourself as a humble, anonymous workman on a Gothic cathedral.

B. Very romantic. Forget it. What I meant originally was that anonymous creation in art, in music or painting or sculpture or theatre, was very unneurotic. And that is the best kind of all, creating unneurotically; which is why the nineteenth-century romantic notion of original genius strikes me as very silly, and as having nothing to do with real creation.

S. But, then, if you're neither the nineteenth-century original genius nor the medieval workman on the cathedral, what third possibility does that leave—something in between?

B. Yes, I am a man making things for use, and highly esteemed as a professional. I am proud of my knowing how to make those things.

S. You were telling me that *Shame* was influenced not so much by the Vietnam war as by your recollections of Hitler's Germany.

B. Yes, exactly. When I was a boy I was in Germany, as a sort of *Austauschjunge* (exchange student) before the war—1935, 1936— and I had German friends; I was fifteen or sixteen years old and came from Sweden completely ignorant, a political virgin. I stayed with the family of a German minister and his four sons and four daughters and a typical German mother in a little village in the interior. I liked them very much. Later, one of the sons, the same age as I, came to Sweden; we spent much time together and I learned German. We were all very fascinated by the fact that he was in the Hitlerjugend, and I went with him to school and they were reading *Mein Kampf* in his religion class; in Weimar, I was at the tenth anniversary of the *Parteitag*. It all held an enormous fascination, and we were all infected by this. Then the war started and I was in the military service; I was drafted from the University and suddenly we realized in Sweden what had happened in Germany; we finally understood. After the war, so many Swedish, Scandinavian, English, and American heroes told us what the

German people should have done under the pressure of the dictatorship, what they really should have done. All these very, very clever people telling us what the German civilians should have been thinking and saying; how they really should have reacted to the concentration camps. All this was terribly painful for me, because I'm not very courageous and I hate physical violence. I don't know how much courage I would have if somebody came to me and said, "Ingmar, you are a very talented man, we like you very much; be the head of the *Schauspielhaus* (National Theatre); if not, you know what will happen to you, your wife, and your children. And, you know, we are having some difficulty with the Jews, and we don't want them in the Theatre; you will fix that for us. If you don't, you know what will happen to you. And I don't know exactly, I don't know at all, how I would have reacted in this situation. That uncertainty was very painful to me, and that is the main problem in *Shame*—what happens to ordinary people in such a war.

S. If I may jump back now to *Persona,* what about those dead bodies in the morgue at the beginning, and the boy who seems to be dead too but then comes to life?

B. It's just my poetry. I was in the hospital; the view out of the window was a chapel where they were carrying out the bodies of the dead, and I knew that house was full of dead people. Of course, I felt it inside me somewhere that the whole atmosphere was one of death, and I felt like that little boy. I was lying there, half dead, and suddenly I started to think of two faces, two intermingled faces, and that was the beginning, the place where it started.

S. And did those two merging faces have a special meaning for you?

B. No, but if I put two faces together, I get this third person.

S. But was one the face of innocence and the other the face of experience?

B. No, nothing like that.

S. Just two faces?

B. Yes, Bibi Andersson and Liv Ullmann didn't know that I did this, that I put them together into one face, and I wanted to give them a surprise, so we made this composite in the laboratory and we got it back to the island where we were and then I asked them to come to the editing room. When they saw those two faces together on the Movieola, Bibi said, "What a terrible picture of you, Liv" and Liv said, "No, it's not me; it's you."

S. And the scene with Gunnar Björnstrand is purely in Alma's imagination; the actual man isn't there?

B. No, it's just a sort of dream.

S. Some critics made terrible fools of themselves by analyzing that as if he were actually there, making love to Alma.

S. Speaking of critics, do you have any afterthoughts about your famous incident with Johnson? [Bergman had hit this critic at an open rehearsal.]

B. No, the only thing is exactly what I said, I hate physical violence.

S. What did this particular critic do to make you so angry?

B. He doesn't believe in what he's doing and he's cynical and he plays a game with other human beings, and I hate this way of behaving. Not of humiliating me, because I know who I am and what I am, but he has a way of humiliating, in a terrible way, the actors. I have seen too much of what he has done to people in this theatre and in other houses.

S. But you're not against criticism in general?

B. No, for heaven's sake, no; we are both acting, don't you think? And, in a way, we are all acting together. Even if we are of different opinions, it doesn't matter. So, in a way, I like to read good criticism, and good criticism is telling me things about . . .

S. Yourself?

B. No, not me, but things I see.

S. Do you read much criticism about your work?

B. I read the reviews in the four Swedish papers, just to get the immediate reaction. But the rest—it takes too much time. You must understand, it's not the reading that takes time, but the effect of it that remains inside you in a very strange way. If it's favorable criticism, it leaves you all atwitter; if it's hostile, you feel poisoned. Just for a few hours, but still, it's a silly waste of time.

S. Let me ask you just one other thing. In *The Naked Night,* at the beginning, when the wagons are arriving in the rain and mud, and suddenly there is the image of a broken-down windmill which is no longer turning; how does that windmill get in there? Do you feel the deliberate need to symbolize some kind of breakdown in human events, or do you happen to be shooting out there and come upon the windmill, and you say, "OK, I'll put the windmill in"?

B. Both. It's always like that when you're creating the right way; you always find things around you that you can use; they seem to be there just for your purpose. It is very strange; suddenly you find things.

BERGMAN
BECOMING BERGMAN

Ingmar Bergman is, in my most carefully considered opinion, the greatest film-maker the world has seen so far. I take film to be a totally visual and totally aural medium—in this ambidextrousness lies its glory—and I consider utterly mistaken the nostalgic sentimentality of those exalters of time past who would put the silent film above the sound, or in any other way minimize the importance of the ear in the enjoyment of film. Although I would not slight the functions of the other senses, I do think vision and audition are the ones by which we communicate best and the most. To the extent that film can make untrammeled use of both those avenues of communication, it can absorb us more masterfully and variously (though not, therefore, more importantly) than any other art, including the theatre, whose visual discourse is somewhat more limited.

Now though a film-maker who masters the visual possibilities of cinema is to be admired, the true lord of the medium is he who controls equally sight and sound, whose word is as good as his image, and, above all, who can manipulate the two in such a way that they reinforce each other and perform in unison or harmony, contrast or counterpoint, at the film-maker's beck. Bergman seems to me the only absolute master to date in both modes, although Fellini in his first films, and Antonioni in a couple of his best, can stand up to him. (So, too, perhaps, can two or three Japanese directors, although utter unfamiliarity with the language makes me hesitant about sweeping pronouncements.) But Bergman has, I firmly believe, achieved the perfect fusion more often than Antonioni and Fellini combined, and he is the only one of the trio whose work continually grows and develops, for whose high-water marks one does not have to turn wistfully backward, for whose present one need not feel apologetic, and to whose future one can look forward with confidence. I have by no means given up hope for Antonioni, but I can face another film by Fellini only with trepidation. And I can find even in a failure of Bergman's, such as *Hour of the Wolf,* more interesting details than in, say, *Fellini Satyricon* or *Zabriskie Point.*

But as Bergman himself says, he did not spring ready-made from Jove's brow, and he had to work on quite a few films before his genuine directorial talent became manifest. And it was not until 1953, with *Gycklarnas Afton,** that Bergman achieved his first masterpiece. He was thirty-five years old. I have not seen the first three films Bergman directed, but I did see the following two, *Night Is My Future* and *Port of Call,* and though the latter has a nice feeling for simple people, neither of them is noteworthy, let alone annunciatory of future greatness.

Before we consider Bergman's work more closely, it may be useful to glance at the misconceptions that have gathered around his name like barnacles and that, to some extent, still crop up among the *pseudodoxia* of our time. Typical of the muddled thinking about Bergman was an article by Caroline Blackwood in the April 1961 issue of *Encounter* entitled "The Mystique of Ingmar Bergman," in which we read, among other things, "Cecil B. de Mille [*sic*] gave the public 'Religion and Sex'; Ingmar Bergman has now simply come up with a more esoteric formula, the Supernatural and Sex, decked out with Symbols." The article concluded: "Maybe by now only the Lord God can deliver [Bergman]—as well as us—from his philosophical ghoulies and ghosties and things that go Bump in the dark." This was a remarkably wrongheaded view even for 1961; but as late as 1964 we find Richard Schickel, now film critic for *Life,* writing in his book *Movies,* "Bergman is both boring and boorish. He is like some distant kin who has turned up at a holiday feast (which is what the cinema ideally is) and insists upon the revelers' attention while he weightily discusses existential questions without ever quite getting to the point." Schickel has since

---

* The awful, exploitative American title of this film, *The Naked Night,* is not to be countenanced. The British title, *Sawdust and Tinsel,* is better, but only the Swedish one, *The Clown's Evening,* conveys Bergman's intentions.

come around to a better way of thinking than this Ancient-Mariner-ish view of Bergman, yet his treatment of him still tends to be grudging—but after all that holiday feasting it must be a little hard to eat crow.

Even as late as June 1970, Andrew Sarris, in his column in the *Village Voice,* complains concerning *A Passion* (*The Passion of Anna*) about "so much undigested clinical material [spewed forth] to so little artistic purpose." We encounter again the old saw about "fumbling metaphysics for which [Bergman's] art is inadequate," and the familiar charge of "obscurity and opacity." There is an in-veterate hatred in movie fans and certain reviewers for films that force them to sit up, concentrate, and think rather than vegetate, soak up trivia, and concoct addled theories about it at leisure. They will go as far as Parker Tyler, that prime purveyor of critical logorrhea, who considers Bergman "disdainful or simply negligent of stating an uncompromisingly personal version of anything." Which is rather like accusing James Joyce of having no personal vision, or Proust of having no personal style.

The superficial, popular notion of Bergman, sparked perhaps by such irresponsible criticism, is as a maker of misty, symbolic, pretentious inscrutabilities (examples: *The Seventh Seal, The Magician*), or tormented sexual battles to the death between bored spouses or neurotic lovers (examples: *Wild Strawberries, Through a Glass Darkly*). There is just enough foundation for this view to make it one of those sinister half-truths that obviate the need for thought. Let me try, before I go into details of individual films, to set the record straight about Bergman's fundamental concerns.

Like most true artists, Bergman is bent on assessing the quality of life: life, which he finds arduous and often insufficient, and death, which he finds not only terrible but also possessed of a terrible fascination. Yet he is also aware of the deep satisfactions to be derived from nature, work, and, above all, love—at least when the weather is good, the work progresses satisfactorily, and love is not corroded by neurosis. There is, to be sure, nothing particularly original about this basic view, except perhaps a somber glow it often gives off—the originality is in the way the vision is embodied, applied—but that makes it all the more recognizably that of a fellow human being, rather than that of a derailed fanatic like Godard, a modish shaman like Pasolini, or a brilliant monomaniac like Bresson.

Bergman has pursued his inquiry into human nature and the

human condition mainly along three lines: (1) Is there a God and an afterlife? If so, of what kind? (2) If the solution to our problems is love between men and women, what kind of love? And how can it be achieved? (3) If we can find peace in work, artistic creation, closeness to nature, the circle of friends or the family circle, just how do we go about accomplishing this? The only type of inquiry that tends to be marginal and implicit in Bergman's films is the social or political—with the important exception of war, which is considered peripherally in such films as *Thirst (Three Strange Loves), The Silence, Persona, A Passion,* and centrally and intensively in *Shame.*

But no film-maker—or novelist, or painter—should be expected to concern himself with all facets of human experience; nor need he examine more than one at a time. Bergman's concerns have shifted from period to period of his life and even, however slightly, from film to film—although connecting threads run through all his works. Thus, for example, the question of God, which was paramount in the films from *The Seventh Seal* to *Winter Light,* is not central to the films before and after, if it arises in them at all; currently, it has ceased to interest Bergman altogether. Another important theme, parents and children, has, conversely, not been bunched together in one period, but crops up intermittently throughout the *oeuvre.* Even the basic form that Robin Wood perceives in "most of Bergman's best films . . . the form of a journey," * is applicable only very loosely to some of the films, and not at all to others. The best films, in fact, do not deal with journeys in the ordinary sense, but they all, without exception, concern interior journeys: journeys into the soul of a character, or into the souls of two or more related characters.

But, differences aside, the sense of continuity in this *oeuvre* is unparalleled in the work of any other film-maker. This continuity is especially apparent in Bergman's more recent films. Though even the early ones were full of his characteristic idiosyncrasies, the later ones truly form fragments of a spiritual autobiography, and could almost, but not quite, be viewed as sections of a *roman fleuve.* The continuity is manifold. It is a continuity of place, such as the island where Bergman now lives, which has become the locale of several of his most recent films. It is also a continuity of faces, those of the excellent repertory company that keeps re-

* *Ingmar Bergman* (New York: Praeger, 1969). Quotations from Wood are always from this monograph.

44

appearing in Bergman's films—some of them almost constantly, others at longer intervals. There is also the consistent dependence on the same technicians, most notably on Sven Nykvist, who has become Bergman's regular cinematographer; and even the persistence of certain devices, such as the minimizing or elimination of the background score to emphasize the dramatic importance of natural sounds and silences.

If we survey briefly the themes of Bergman's principal films, not only do we get a clearer picture of his preoccupations and of the interconnectedness of the films, but also we can understand and evaluate more fully the place and achievement of the four particular films this study is concerned with. In *Prison* (stupidly renamed *The Devil's Wanton*), we find the doomed prostitute Birgitta-Carolina, a girl who can do nothing but be exploited, suffer, and kill herself—a crude symbol of the helplessness of the simple soul. Counterpointing and sometimes meshing with this theme is that of Tomas, the writer-journalist, who fights with his wife, Sofi, but, after an unsuccessful dalliance with Birgitta-Carolina, goes back to Sofi for better or worse. And there is the frame story of Martin, the film director, who considers making a film suggested to him by a former teacher, Paul, just released from a mental institution, and dealing with the Devil as the lord of the world making human life a continuous hell on earth. In the end of the frame story, Martin declares that such a film cannot be made, because it would end with a question instead of a solution.

But, ironically, the more independent and secure Bergman was to become, the more his films became open-ended, abutting on unanswered and perhaps unanswerable questions, and the more, we are free to conclude, they are depictions of a world ruled by the Devil. His first words upon coming to power, according to Paul's projected film in *Prison,* were: "I command that everything shall continue as before." In *Thirst,* for which Bergman did not write the screenplay, but which is as Bergmanesque as any of his films, the principal couple, Bertil and Rut, remain together even though they bore and exasperate each other to the point of attempted murder. "I don't want to be alone and independent," says Bertil, finding that to be worse "than the hell we are living in. After all, we have each other." Viola, the other principal character, is alone; a born victim, she is rejected by her lover, widowed, and both her analyst and an old girl friend she meets again want merely to seduce her. She drowns herself. There are two hells on earth,

Bergman is saying in this interesting early film: one is called Together; the other is called Alone, and it is the worse of the two.

These films date from 1949; 1950 saw the coming of what is
generally thought to be Bergman's first fully achieved film, *Summerplay* (as it should be called, or *Summer Games,* but not *Illicit
Interlude,* as it was released here). This film, which Bergman considers his first mature work, is one that I have never been able to
accept as a whole. A superficial reason for this might be that Mai-
Britt Nilsson lacks the depth and plasticity of some other Bergman
leading ladies. A more serious trouble with *Summerplay* is that it
is one of those films in which Bergman tries to come up with an
answer rather than merely ask his disturbing, extremely important
questions, and, as I already noted, his answer films are weaker
than his question films.

The question in *Summerplay* is, broadly speaking, how to make
life prevail in the face of encroaching death; and also, if one is an
artist, how to make art enhance rather than enslave one's existence. The heroine, Marie, is a ballerina, withdrawn and embittered
by the tragic end of her first love. This was a summer romance
in the Archipelago with Henrik, a young student whom she was
going to marry, but who died at summer's end in consequence of
an ill-judged dive into shallow water. After this, Marie drifts into a
strange relationship with a mildly sinister uncle, Erland, formerly
her mother's lover, and becomes a successful but unhappy ballerina. She is now involved with David, a journalist, but finds him less
poetic than Henrik, which indeed he is. As the film begins, Erland
has sent to Marie Henrik's journal, which he had confiscated before Marie could find it. She now reads it for the first time, then
goes back on a pilgrimage to the island where she and Henrik were
lovers. People and sights there bring back the past: troubled,
idealistic, frantic, tragic, and, above all, sweet. Erland appears,
too, revealing in himself the ravages of loneliness, and when Marie
returns to the Stockholm Opera, the ballet master confronts her
with some hard truths. She gets David to read Henrik's diary. As
the film ends, Marie has relived and absorbed her past, incorpo-
rated a little of Henrik's spirit in the matter-of-fact David, embraced
her work with greater acceptance, and is now able to face the
future more resolutely and contentedly.

The difficulty with this film, very much as with *The Seventh Seal,
Wild Strawberries,* or *Through a Glass Darkly,* is that the words
and images of lost happiness and of despair at its loss are far too

strong for the conciliatory, resigned or optimistic, *volte-face* to cancel out. At the nadir of her fortunes, Marie becomes her uncle's mistress, and Erland answers her anguished questioning with, "No, my little one, there is nothing that, in the long run, has any meaning." Whereupon Marie, with icy calm, declares, "I do not believe that God exists. And if he does, I hate him. If he stood before me, I'd spit in his face. . . . I shall hate him till the day I die." This scene, in Erland's cloistered apartment, with darkness falling and Erland promising to teach Marie how to immure herself within her skin, is so terrifying, coming as it does after the summer idyll that ends in disaster, that nothing afterward can quite break its somber spell. Later, the ballet master, dressed as Dr. Coppelius, reinforces the gloom by his insistence on uncompromising dedication to one's work and no further rewards after retirement.

Over against this, however, we are given the final image of hope: David, presumably softened by his reading of the diary, watches from the wings Marie dancing the role of Odette in *Swan Lake.* She comes off stage and, raising herself *en pointes,* kisses David, and then, on the same toes that lift her to art as to love, dances out on stage, where, in the ballet, love frees the heroine from the wicked magician's power. It is a fine image, but does it convey the "idea that one must fully confront and embrace one's despair before it is possible to move beyond it," as Robin Wood interprets the sense of the film, or even, as Jörn Donner puts it, that "when she has relived everything, [Marie] can both forget and remember in the right way, that is . . . go on living"? * That, certainly, is what the film is about, that "there is no other answer except to go on living," as Donner puts it, but has the acceptability, let alone the exhilaration, of this stoicism been sufficiently dramatized and visualized in the closing passages of the film? I think not.

From this point in Bergman's development we can look back at his various themes and see them converge on his first masterpiece, which we are now ready to examine, skipping over such interesting but lesser films as *Summer with Monika* and *Women Waiting* (*Secrets of Women*), with its brilliant third episode in the stalled elevator. The year is 1953, and the film is *The Clown's Evening.*

---

* Jörn Donner, *The Personal Vision of Ingmar Bergman* (Bloomington: Indiana University Press, 1964). The Swedish edition appeared two years earlier.

THE CLOWN'S EVENING (THE NAKED NIGHT)

In the April 1960 *Esquire,* James Baldwin published an interview with Bergman, in the course of which the film-maker once again named *Summerplay* as his favorite film. "It is probably not Bergman's best movie," Baldwin commented. "I would give that place to . . . *The Naked Night* (which should really be called *The Clown's Evening*). . . . [It] is the most blackly ambivalent of Bergman's films—and surely one of the most brutally erotic movies ever made—but it is essentially a study of the masculine helplessness before the female force." As late as 1964, Dwight Macdonald still saw *The Clown's Evening* as Bergman's masterpiece, and its theme as being the acceptance of life, the "coming to some sort of terms with it, however meager." "In the final analysis," writes Peter Cowie, "it is a film about tolerance, tolerance in all its perplexing disguises." * For Jörn Donner, the basic point is that "life can be lived by him who sees the greatness of the moment," which strikes me as nonsense; but Donner seems right when he identifies "the humiliation theme" as "the central one in the film." Robin Wood finds the film remarkable especially for its communication of "pain, both mental and physical, [which] is centered in sex, where the human being is most sensitive, where the greatest damage can be done and the pain of existence is felt most strongly." Clearly a complex film, which elicits various, often conflicting, interpretations, and arouses antithetical pronouncements, from Mac-

* *Sweden 2* (New York: A. S. Barnes & Co., 1970). All quotations from Cowie are from this book.

Dawn; the journeying circus. Albert, the ringmaster, and Frost, the clown, ride in the wagon in which Albert's girl, Anne, lies asleep. Frost's story begins.

The regiment was shooting by the shore.

*The story: Near Frost's circus a company of soldiers
are on maneuvers. His wife, Alma, goes to see the
troops.*

donald's "masterpiece" to Pauline Kael's "*The Naked Night* is powerful all right, but I think it's powerfully awful."

The Clown's Evening is the story of Albert Johansson, owner of a seedy traveling circus, the Cirkus Alberti, and of Anne, his mistress. The film covers twenty-four hours in their life, between a dawn and a dawn. Albert wakes up inside the wagon he shares with Anne, tucks her in, and clambers onto the driver's seat of the lead wagon. As they are approaching the town where Albert's abandoned wife, Agda, lives with their two young boys, old Jens, the coachman, tells the story of something that happened hereabouts seven years ago. Frost, the principal clown of the Cirkus Alberti, and his wife, Alma, were then with another circus. One day, Alma was parading in front of a regiment on maneuvers on a beach.* The officers, on a dare, get her to strip naked and go bathing with the soldiery; they laugh obscenely as they watch it happen. A boy is dispatched, cruelly, to fetch Frost. The gangly, pathetic clown arrives at the seashore, followed by guffawing circus people, and is mocked and laughed at by the military. He is afraid of the water and begs his nude, cavorting wife to come out. She taunts him until he sheds his costume and wades in to get her. The boy hides both Frost's and Alma's clothes, and the undergarmented Frost must now carry his naked wife in front of the exhilarated regiment and try to cover her nudity with his body. The terrain is rocky and harsh on Frost's bare feet; twice he stumbles, the sec-

* The script, which departs more than usual from the actual film, has the regiment building a bridge in the bay. There is no evidence of this on screen.

52

ond time without being able to rise. Alma is overcome with remorse and solicitude, and keeps holding on to him pitifully as the circus people carry him spread-eagled toward their tents. By the time Jens finishes his tale, Albert has fallen asleep, even though the anecdote emblematically prefigures his own story.

The circus arrives in town, and the tent has to be raised in the now pouring rain. With half their costumes pawned in the town they just played, their only wild animal a sick and emaciated bear, they themselves starving, the circus people are in bad shape. Albert dreams of the affluence and glory of circuses in America. He decides to go into town and borrow some costumes from Sjuberg, the director of the local theatre. Anne is to make herself as pretty as possible—Sjuberg likes good-looking women—but he, Albert will be there to protect her if things threaten to go too far. (This remark is to prove doubly ironic.) At the theatre, Albert and Anne are awed by the for them sumptuous and romantic ambience of a playhouse with a rehearsal in progress. They shuffle about awkwardly on the bright stage, from which Albert timidly addresses his request to a Sjuberg divined somewhere in the dark auditorium. Sjuberg comes up on the stage, insults the pair, but instructs Blom, the janitor, to take the couple to the storage rooms upstairs and have them pick up what they need; the payment is an invitation for the entire theatre company to the circus's opening night.

While Anne preens in front of a full-length mirror as she tries on various costumes (Albert and Blom are off in some other part of the attic), she is suddenly seized by the shoulders. It is Frans, the *jeune premier* of the company, who has been observing her for some time: he must have her, by seduction, rape, or even marriage. A battle of words ensues, and Anne, after humiliating Frans, agrees to kiss him once if he will bang his head against the floor. But she

The men offer her a hatful of money.

*Alma goes swimming nude, to the derision and
delight of the men. Someone fetches the clown, and
as he faces the scene, he screams out her name;
an anguished silent scream. (There is no sound track
for this portion of the film.)*

With a crowd of jeering and laughing soldiers
looking on, Frost tries to cover his wife's shame
and his own.

Frost's humiliation. He collapses under his burden. (See Persona, *page 254.)*

The circus people bring him home.

gives him only a hint of a kiss, pulls away, and leaves with Albert, who has reappeared. There follows a scene missing from American prints of the film, in which the circus people parade through the town advertising their opening, only to have the police confiscate their horses, which reduces the performers to pulling the wagons back themselves under the jeers of the populace.

In the afternoon, Albert is about to visit his wife and children, whom he hasn't seen in three years. Anne is jealous, afraid that Albert wants an out and will resettle with his family. As he gets ready to leave, she nastily warns that he will not find her there on his return. He sneers: "Where would you go?" and leaves. We see him next clumsily confronting his older boy in Agda's tobacco shop, then accepting the invitation to share a homely meal with his wife. A warm friendliness seems at first to re-establish itself. She finds that Albert's jacket is missing a button and insists on sewing it on; when Albert reluctantly removes his coat, he is revealed wearing only a dickey and cuffs, and his dire poverty emerges. She offers to lend him money. He won't accept it, and accuses her of trying to get even for his deserting her. It turns out that she is a prosperous tobacconist, much happier away from the circus. As they drink cognac in the silent room, the image dissolves into Anne's sneaking into the theatre, watching with great emotional responsiveness Frans rehearsing a grandiloquent suicide scene, and then entering his dressing room.

There follows an extraordinary scene of sadomasochistic maneuvering, of compliments mixed with insults, and of violence that merely apes passion. Since Frans now seems unwilling to take Anne with him, and inasmuch as he has locked her in with him and refuses to give her the key, she agrees to go to bed with him in exchange for a golden amulet which, he says, will enable her to live independently for at least a year. They make love vehemently. From Anne's act of unfaithfulness we dissolve back to Albert and Agda. (The dissolves are beautifully managed, with the face of one woman slowly and significantly mutating into that of the other, so different and so differently engaged. This device significantly foreshadows *Persona*.) The smaller son now obtains his father's last coin to get the street organ-grinder and his monkeys to perform for him. Albert summons up his courage and asks Agda to take him back: he could be useful to the business. She refuses, preferring her orderly world, of whose tranquillity the restless Albert would deprive her. He accepts a little money, at last, and leaves, shamefaced.

Lust having turned to pure coldness, Anne takes the piece of jewelry from Frans and leaves. In the square, we see the organ-grinder and his monkeys again. The wretched Albert notices Anne coming out of the theatre and hurrying into a jewelry store. When she emerges after a long period, she seems shaken. Back in the wagon, Albert wrests the truth from Anne, who has, in turn, guessed what he was up to and what the outcome was. Anne claims that Frans forced her to submit. But Albert saw the initial encounter between Frans and Anne, and knows that she wants to get away as much as he does. They are now as cognizant of their joint and individual helplessness as of their respective infidelities. In the script, Albert laughs and Anne exclaims: "Don't laugh like that. *Albert:* We are wedged in, Anne. Chained together. *Anne:* I'll go away. *Albert:* You'll go away! What can you do besides riding bare-

Bergman cuts to the Cirkus Alberti arriving at its latest pitch. Now Anne and Albert's story begins.

To whom is Blom jabbering
during rehearsals?

Onstage: Albert and Anne enter the local theatre.

back and performing tricks on a carpet. They wouldn't hire you as a maid."

Presently Frost comes in and he and Albert proceed to get drunk together. Then Albert produces a gun, with which, he proclaims, he will do a humane deed. Kill himself? Certainly not; perhaps kill the sickly bear. Frost exclaims: "But don't forget to kill Alma as well, it would be an act of kindness." The two men tumble out into the open and mingle with the circus folk. Albert has a fit in which he alternates between cursing Anne and reaffirming his compassion and need for her.

Opening night. The clowns perform their routines, all of which consist of humiliating the patsy. The actors from the theatre arrive just as Anne, gotten up as a Spanish equestrienne, is to go into her bareback riding act. As she circles around the little arena, Frans (sitting next to a young actress) begins to show off by shouting crude jokes about their intimacy. Albert controls himself until someone tosses a firecracker and causes Anne to be thrown by her horse. Now Albert, with his ringmaster's whip, twice in a row knocks off Frans's straw hat; it rolls into the arena. Fuming, Frans comes down to retrieve it, and is kicked in the rear by Albert. Sjuberg jumps up and declares that a duel is in order. The fight is terrible. Though the hulking Albert is clearly stronger than the dandified Frans, the latter is a much more skilled fighter, and a dirty one, too. At the crucial moment he kicks sawdust into the already bloodied and blindly swinging Albert's eyes, and ends up by kneeing him in the groin and reducing him to a pulp. Like a fury, Anne hurls herself at Frans and deeply scratches his face.

Anne meets Frans in the mirror. Bergman makes
frequent use of mirrors in his films to express various
levels of reality. (See Smiles of a Summer Night,
page 126, and Persona, *page 283.)*

They are separated: Albert is carried off to his wagon; the show is over.

Partly recovered from the beating, Albert chases everyone from the wagon, locks himself in, and grabs the gun again. He sits in front of the mirror, tries to shoot himself, but the gun misfires. He lacks the courage to try once more; instead, he shoots his image in the mirror. He lunges out, presently, among the terrified circus people, and, despite Alma's pathetic protest, proceeds to shoot the bear. Then he rushes to the stables and, his head pressed against his favorite horse, he cries himself into appeasement. He notices that a hoof needs reshoeing, and as he starts issuing commands, life comes back into the man. He orders the departure of the circus.

It is night again and the wagons are rolling. Frost and Albert are walking alongside them, and the clown tells about a dream he has had. In it, his wife told him he needed rest, and, with his consent, turned him into a fetus and took him into her womb. He fell asleep there, rocked as in a cradle, and grew smaller and smaller. "Finally I was no bigger than a seed, and then I was gone altogether." Now Alma's voice, her real voice, is heard, gruffly summoning Frost into their wagon. "She can't sleep without me by her side," he explains apologetically, and goes in. Already there is a promise of dawn in the sky. Suddenly Anne is seen, waiting for Albert. They exchange a meaningful glance, a half-smile, and walk on together toward daybreak.

The Clown's Evening is the first Bergman film to utilize a framework of dreams, or dreamlike occurrences, a pattern that recurs, with some variations, in The Seventh Seal, Wild Strawberries, Persona, and Shame. In this case, the first episode, Jens's tale about Frost and Alma, is not really a dream, but the one flashback in the film, presented in such an unusual way, looking so different from the rest of the movie, and impinging only so dimly on Albert's consciousness, that it very much resembles a waking dream Albert might be having. (Significantly, some writers erroneously recall this episode as a dream; thus Ado Kyrou in Le Surréalisme au cinéma, and Eric Rohmer, who refers to it as "a short and strange dream sequence before which even Buñuel pales.") Whether flashbacks or dreams, the two Frost-Alma episodes frame the film. The first shows a man humiliated, indeed crucified, by his wife, but a wife who then shares in the humiliation and is filled with repentance and humility. The final dream is exactly the opposite of this: here the woman is the great mother into whom the man crawls for peace, oblivion, death. So the double aspect of the man-woman relationship, which is the main theme of the film, appears emblematically at its beginning and end. Upon closer inspection, this doubleness is already suggested at the outset, in the brief sequence in which Albert climbs out of the bed he seems to have shared happily with Anne, covers the sleeping girl solicitously but looks at her with a certain anxiety before leaving the wagon. At film's end, the duality is more conspicuous: Frost's peaceful dream is followed by Alma's peremptory summons and the clown's sheepish attempt to justify his servile obedience.

This betokens a mature film-maker's ability to round out his film, to make episodes balance one another meaningfully, not just for the sake of geometric design. Notice: in the beginning, it is the

Please don't go!

*Albert and Anne are trapped
together in their life. Bergman
has shot Albert from a low angle
to show him in a confined space.
Albert leaves. Bergman uses
doors expressively in many of
his films. Bergman: "It's fascinating. A door separates you
from other people, or you can
open it and come in."*

short, deceptive tenderness of the tucking in that is overshadowed
by the long, shocking flashback; hence the note of pessimism pre-
ponderates. In the end, the merely narrated dream of peace carries less weight than the imperious, dramatized summoning that
succeeds it, but is then reinforced by the final image of Albert's
and Anne's coming together. The disparate, warring ingredients
are here again, but in significantly altered proportions and with a
different rhythm.

But the rhythmic interplay is not merely thematic; it is also visual. Thus there is a knowing alternation of outdoor and indoor
scenes (the former photographed by Hilding Bladh, the latter by
Sven Nykvist), of brightly lit and predominantly dark sequences.
This does not mean, however, that the dark scenes are to be
equated with unhappiness, and vice versa, although dark scenes
abound, as does a brooding, gloomy atmosphere. Yet the film is
not "one of the blackest of Bergman's," as Pauline Kael would
have it, a piece of "heavy, mawkish expressionism circa 1920."

There are delicate ironies as well as deeply upsetting moments; and the ending is one of resignation tinged with a modest hope, rather like the ending of *Thirst,* with its recognition that hell together is better than hell alone. Here the conciliatory effect is not only in the couple's continuing side by side; it is also in the long shots of the circus, financially reprieved, rolling on, and in the visually and emotionally satisfying light in the sky; whether it is daybreak or merely the midnight sun scarcely matters.

The opening sequences of the film exemplify this alternation of light and dark. The initial shots are of the dim but not black northern night tending toward dawn; this is followed by the darkling interior of the wagon. This, in turn, is followed by the harsh glare in which the flashback unfurls. The exaggerated blacks and whites, with very little transitional gray, suggest not only the imperfectly recollected landscape of memory, but also a kind of schematically simplified world in which black and white, good and evil, rub against each other in merciless contiguity. Alma is seen arriving

*Albert tries to come into his wife Agda's world,
but he is not of it. His finery is not true to him; when
he takes off his jacket, his shirt is only a fake front.
His massive animal self is revealed as he sits in his
false cuffs. He sweats in Agda's cool world.*

on the soldier-infested beach in a medium-to-long shot, at which distance she still looks fairly pretty; during the naked bathing she is seen in extreme long shot, so that the full pathos of her nudity and age hits us simultaneously and in close-up only later on, when she and Frost start their humiliating recession. Thus size of image becomes as important as lighting.

Bergman is also one of the great masters of the sound track, quick to realize how much is gained by using music sparingly (later he was to abandon it altogether), and by using natural sounds, both realistically and expressionistically, to the utmost degree. In *The Clown's Evening* he had, for the first and last time, the collaboration of the most distinguished Swedish composer, Karl-Birger Blomdahl. In this flashback scene, for example, there is only one distorted sort of melody that is superseded by an orchestration of cannons going off at regular intervals, raucous laughter from the military, and later, during Frost's calvary, drum rolls. Sometimes the horror is increased by showing the laughing mouths in close-up, but with no audible sound. The silences are occasionally punctuated by Jens's voice droning on, and twice there is speech: first, when Frost is told about what is happening; next, when an officer issues a command to start firing the cannons. These bits of dialogue serve as a sort of diapason for the scene, from harsh irony to plain brutality. When the boy summons Frost to the beach in the name of the regiment, the clown at first thinks

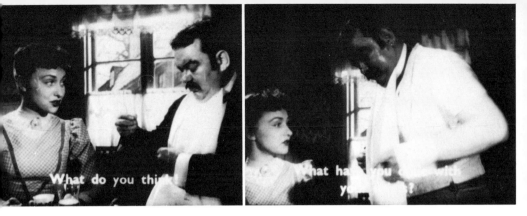

they want to honor him; when he finds out what it is all about, the script has him loudly and terribly cursing God. In the film, the sound has stopped again, and the silent curse or cry of pain, one cannot be sure which, is probably more heart-rending than anything we could actually hear. It is the interplay, then, of cannonade and cachinnation, drums and silence, narration and bits of dialogue, that creates the aural *dépaysement* of this episode.

But Bergman uses equally many brilliant visual devices. The cannons provide Rabelaisianly exaggerated phallic symbols. The clown, carrying his wife up a rocky gradient, his bare feet getting wounded and stumbling under the burden, becomes an almost too glaring image of Calvary. But it should be remarked that the cross he is carrying is his wife: a very special kind of calvary, and one of the dominant themes of the film. Let us recall here Donner's and Wood's observations about the humiliation motif: a sexual humiliation, hitting the victim where he is most vulnerable—in the groin. It is, of course, the Strindbergian theme of the battle of the sexes; but no one has explored it on screen so ruthlessly and illuminatingly as Ingmar Bergman has. The clown's garb, dropped on the ground outside the tent at the end of the scene and left lying spread-eagled, is a final, abject form of crucifixion in effigy.

Vernon Young poses the problem of the "overbearing intensity" with which both Strindberg and Bergman engage the problem of man-woman relations: "August Strindberg with mysogyny almost unsurpassed, Bergman with a degree of solicitation so morbid as to make us wonder if it might not conceal a secretly rooted enmity." Young is, I think, being excessively clever about something quite obvious: Bergman, as this Frost-Alma episode illustrates, shows man both deeply solicitous of and helplessly bound to woman, but I am not ready to perceive this as morbid, nor would I produce the decrepit Freudian rabbit of a "secretly rooted enmity" with such an air of superiority from an old hat. Certainly any great passion contains the seeds of its opposite, and adoration, as we all know, can easily turn into hate. But there is nothing "secretly rooted" about this—at least no more secret than the obverse is on a coin. It is just the old concept of love-hate examined by Bergman with extraordinary lucidity and unstinting vigor.

Frost and Alma are the crude model for the Albert-Anne relationship, which this rather short film (ninety minutes) manages to capture in awe-inspiring completeness. As Albert wakes up in the early morning, he looks at Anne, according to the screenplay, "as if he wanted to break through the barrier of this smooth white

Albert caught between two worlds. A long dissolve from Agda's face (see first picture, page 68), calm in the clock-ticking silence, to Anne, tensely observing Frans from the wings of the theatre. She sees . . .

forehead and read her dreams." I am reminded here of Büchner's Danton speaking to his beloved wife, Julie: "We know little about one another. We are thick-skinned creatures; we stretch out our hands for each other, but it's wasted effort: we just rub off some of the other's tough hide—we are very lonely." This could well be the epigraph for *The Clown's Evening*. But something else, too, is promptly suggested: in the way the bearish, coarse-looking Albert Johansson kisses Anne's lovely shoulder and proceeds to tuck her in, "We see his anxious solicitude for her which is also," as Robin Wood notes, "a sort of uneasy possessiveness." The problem of these lovers is partly the difficulty of understanding another person, the inadequacy of the human sensorium and, as it were, of the

72

Frans committing suicide. Anne is taken in.

human condition itself; but it is also the desire for possession, domination, and its attendant courting of humiliation.

When Alma accepts the invitation to go bathing with the men, the temptation is only partly the money they have collected in a cap; it is as much, one feels, the terrible insecurity that takes hold of a beautiful woman at the approach of age. And the overexposed film in this episode suggests both the heat of the day and the quality of overripeness, of film and flesh past their primes. And after what might be called the basic-human-weakness motif comes that of humiliation: first the separate ridiculing of Alma and Frost, then their joint humiliation as they are exposed in their physical and spiritual nudity. In the case of Albert and Anne, the external cause of their difficulties is the pennilessness of the circus, but this is quickly followed by the humiliation motif: their insensitive, exploitative treatment of the other person. This begins with Albert's refusal to reassure Anne that he will not desert her (and, indeed, he contemplates leaving), and with his use of her as bait to get costumes out of Sjuberg. It continues with Anne's and Frans's little game, watched by Albert (as we learn later) but without his daring to put a stop to it for fear the costume deal might fall through. More explicitly, the humiliation motif is sounded in Sjuberg's insulting remarks to Albert and Anne, and his contempt for circus performers in general, mixed in with which there is also a good deal of contempt for actors, *i.e.,* self-contempt. To heighten Anne's and Albert's discomfiture before Sjuberg, there are, as Peter Cowie observes, "the footlights exposing their pitiful rig-out, and the low camera angles," which show them in distorting perspective.

74

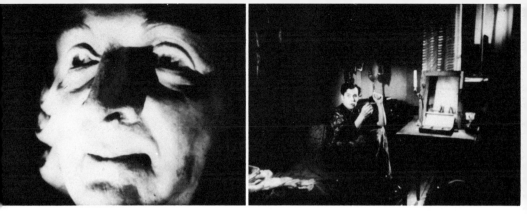

At this point, let me quote Sjuberg's speech as an early example of Bergman's verbal mastery. "Why shouldn't I insult you? You put up with it, you don't punch me in the jaw. We despise you because you live in wagons and we in dirty hotel rooms; we produce art, and you offer stunts and tricks. The plainest and least gifted of us can spit on the best of you. Why? Because you stake your lives and we our vanity. I think you look ridiculous and patched, sir, and your little lady would surely be much more fun without her gaudy rags. If you only had the courage, you would find us even more ridiculous, with our fake elegance, our painted faces, our affected speech. Why shouldn't I insult you?" Consider the subtlety and multivalence of the central statement: "Because you stake your lives and we our vanity." On the lowest level, this merely establishes the opposition of life and art, the hostility of people who trade in one currency toward those who trade in another. But it also implies the superiority of art to life, so that death is insignificant compared to artistic failure. It further suggests the importance of satisfying one's ego—vanity—without which life is worse than no life at all. But there is perhaps also the suggestion that highbrow values are perverted if they can so glibly subordinate life to art; the circus people at least recognize life as the greatest good, but only—poor, desperate fools!—in order to gamble with it. So the statement seems to resolve itself into perfect cynicism: those who commit themselves less can lord it over the foolish wretches who have to stake everything.

From the moment Frans hurls himself at Anne, another theme asserts itself, a theme whose visual expression permeates the film: self-absorption, narcissism, play-acting before a mirror. The mirror becomes an extension of the stage, framing as it does a face in a miniature proscenium for the benefit of a small but select audi-

For shame

*Anne is impressed with Frans and his world and
with what she considers is her power over him.
Thinking to free herself from Albert and the circus,
she makes love to him in exchange for a fake amulet
he cruelly tempts her with. Violent eroticism based
on false premises leaves Anne . . .*

ence, oneself and perhaps one other person, both of whom one wishes to impress with one's performance. Anne is primping before the mirror in borrowed finery when Frans pounces on her, and the ensuing scene often shows one or the other of them reflected in the mirror. Later, when Anne comes to Frans's dressing room, and Frans teaches her how to make up her face, the mirror again takes over. But the flattering mirror can—like the stage, for that matter—become the teller of harsh truth, as when Albert, having been defeated in the arena and humiliated by Frans, sees his bloated, bloodied, begrimed face in the glass and wants to shoot himself, but, after one aborted attempt, has only enough courage to shoot his mirror image. As I wrote in *Acid Test:* "All the stages in the seduction of Anne . . . are viewed in a mirror: it is as if some vainer, less real, less responsible self lived in mirrors. It takes over, acts for you, and can be blamed for whatever happens. Consequently, when Anne's shamed common-law husband . . . attempts to blow his brains out, he ends by shooting his reflection in a mirror: the scapegrace self that gets you entangled becomes the scapegoat self that dies to set you free." This scene was prefigured when the drunken Albert threatens to shoot Frost in the head—Frost who is a mirror image of himself—and the clown, seemingly contemptuous of life until then, suddenly begins to cling

But no one shall take my peace of
mind and freedom away!

totally separate.
To show Albert and Anne cast back upon themselves,
Bergman intercuts Albert as he finds himself back
on the road and Anne cast off by Frans.

Anne is playing solitaire as Albert enters. (Bergman uses this exact composition—the enigmatic figure in silhouette entering a darkened interior—in The Magician.) *They are separate yet bound together by what they have done to each other in their efforts to escape their condition.*
Violent confrontation shatters their separateness as they shout out their anger and grief. (See Persona.)

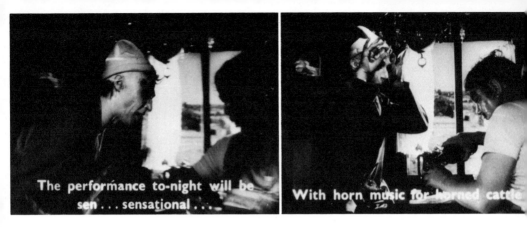

The performance to-night will be sen . . . sensational . . .

With horn music for horned cattle

In the confines of the wagon, Frost makes fun of
Albert and thus of himself.
Frost: "The performance tonight will be sensational,
with horn music for horned cattle."

to it desperately, precisely what Albert is going to do later on. And after Albert has shot his image in the glass without obtaining full emotional relief, he goes out to shoot the sickly old bear, yet another reflection of the dilapidated circus director. But—so intertwined are Bergman's themes—the shooting of the bear is also an act of revenge on women, for the bear was Alma's special pet, and Bergman's camera, instead of showing the death of the beast, brilliantly concentrates on Alma's deathlike collapse along the bars of the cage, as if the bullets had struck her.

As important as the themes of humiliation and of the mirrored self is the theme of entrapment and attempted escape. Both Albert and Anne feel imprisoned in their relationship as well as in their mode of existence. Albert has become separated from his wife, Agda, who, though in love with him, could not tolerate the life of the circus—especially when Albert started training their two small boys in circus skills. Now a successful tobacconist, financially far more secure than her husband, with her children there beside her, Agda exudes an inner peace. Albert, visiting her, is overcome with nostalgia for the placid, sedentary life. Or is it only stagnation? Consider this significant exchange: "*Albert:* What silence! *Agda:* Yes, it's a quiet street. *Albert:* Everything is alike: summer and winter; year in, year out. Nothing stirs. *Agda:* For me, it's a ripening. *Albert:* For me, it's emptiness." It is probably too strong to speak, as Jörn Donner does, of "the spiritual death she radiates," but

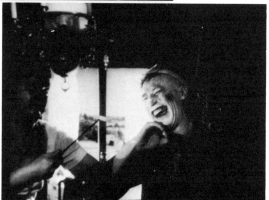

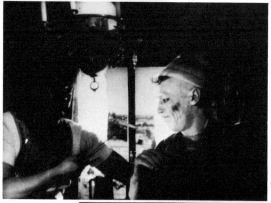

The confined space grows tighter.
Albert: "I should shoot you, Frosty!"

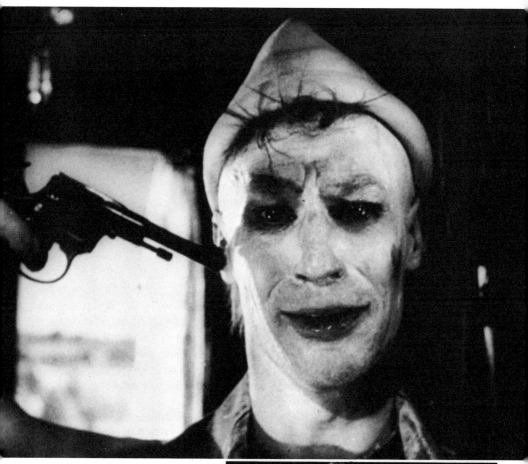
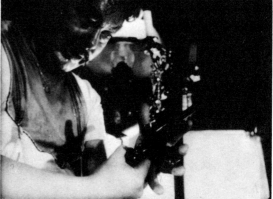

*The tension snaps, hurtling the drunken Albert and
Frost out of the dark, close wagon and talk of death
into the open air and the life of the sunlit world.
Albert: "What a life! Look at the life around us."*

*Bergman often uses this contrast between outside
and inside, confinement and freedom, darkness and
light, for instance in* Persona *on pages 256 and 257,
for a different effect.*

Agda certainly represents the kind of physical and spiritual comfort the harried artist yearns for but would find deadening were he
to achieve it—which, in any case, is most unlikely. When Albert
nevertheless tries to persuade Agda to take him back, she rebuffs
him: "I don't want to have you around here. This is my world, my
very own: orderly, well-kept—an ordinary life. I want to keep this
for myself. . . . No one will rob me of my peace of mind, my clean
life." The solid middle-class woman ultimately rejects the restless
artist, even if for a while she loved him.

Anne, too, wishes to escape the nomadic, impoverished life with
Albert and the Cirkus Alberti. But her bid to get Frans to take her
with him fails for several reasons. Anne, as Albert has pointed out
to her, is not trained for anything beyond what she is doing; Frans,
the narcissistic actor, cannot care for anyone but himself; and, by
strong implication, the stage actor feels infinitely superior to the
itinerant circus mountebank. There is an ugly mixture of snobbish
condescension and unholy curiosity in Frans's question to Anne,
whom he has just locked into his dressing room: "You who are in
the circus, can you tell me how you get the bear to dance? I have
heard tell that you use bars of red-hot iron." Even if what Frans

What a life! Look at all the life around us!

implies was true—and it might be—is he not using an equally ugly method to seduce a human being? Or is a circus performer only an animal? One thinks of the parallel between Albert and the bear —and also, more remotely, of a film yet to come, *The Seventh Seal,* in which the villainous Raval, at knife point and with the approval of the crowd, forces the actor Jof to dance like a bear. Frans finally obtains Anne for a worthless trinket and, not content with this, humiliates her publicly by broadcasting the fact that he has been riding her (as she does her horse) to the circus crowd. But the most important parallel is to what Frans finally does to Albert: with blows and kicks and sawdust in his eyes, Albert is reduced by Frans to a pathetic dancing bear, swaying and tottering and tumbling in his misery, entertaining the rabble with his humiliation and pain.

The inexorable fate of the traveling performer is to be chained to his life no less than to his bed partner. There is no way open to him either into the bourgeoisie or into a more stable and socially accepted form of performance, the theatre. By showing Anne and Albert's triple failure—with each other, with their profession, with their sociosexual escape routes—Bergman conveys a profound existential gloom. Yet here, too, as at the end of *Thirst* and *Summerplay,* there is a sense of possible redemption—or, at least, of mitigation of suffering—through sticking it out together. And indeed the unity of the couple Albert-Anne becomes manifest under the pressure of persecution, just as that of Frost and Alma did before them. When Frans publicly insults Anne, Albert comes to her defense. That the defense fails, and that, in defending her honor, he is clearly also defending his own, is less important than that he fights for his woman with all the rage of a provoked bull. Similarly,

A long shot pulls back from "the life around us" still farther to create an awareness of the transiency of the circus and our smallness in the world. (See page 60; Smiles of a Summer Night, *page 132; and* Winter Light, *page 190) From his, a cut back into life . . .*

when Frans, by skill and dirty tricks, beats the much heavier Albert to a pulp, Anne furiously comes to Albert's defense. Here, again, it matters less that she is the initially offended party than that she hurls herself at her lover's tormentor, to quote the beautiful irony in the screenplay, "like a fury, like a true Spanish woman."

A word on the literary brilliance of this screenplay is again in order. Take this comment on Anne, who has been doing her bareback-riding act dressed as a Spaniard (in imitation of the famous Lola Montez, no doubt), but who now, under stress, truly becomes what she has been merely faking. To put such a penetratingly witty observation into a stage direction argues that Bergman is as much a writer as a film-maker. And consider this description of the crowd at the circus: "They laugh readily, sweat a good deal, and send comments whirling round the ears of the artistes. They are having fun like honest folk who have the right to amuse themselves in the evening, when a day of work is done." Here, again, Bergman's delicate irony might seem wasted, for no one actually voices it in the film. But whether or not he thinks of the screen play as something that will be published, Bergman clearly thinks in such writerly terms, and into the scenario they go, regardless of who, if anyone, will read them. In fact, all the descriptive passages in Bergman's screenplays (as we shall have ample opportunity to see) are on an imaginative and linguistic par with what is actually seen and heard on screen. And that, it cannot be stressed often enough, is the equal of our best fiction and drama.

In the almost unconscious, spontaneous solidarity between Anne and Albert, the final reconciliation—or, at any rate, resignation—is prepared for. Thus the final coming together is longer a *deus ex machina,* but ushered in, first, by the sentimentally weepy, drunken, but not ungenuine access of pity Albert has for Anne and himself; then by the couple's sticking up for each other with fist and nail; lastly, both by the scene between Frost and Albert, in which the former relates his uxorious dream and is promptly summoned to his wife's side, and by the image of the circus wagons moving indomitably into the future.

At this point it is proper to examine the film's visual language, the impact of its imagery. Compared to the intense brilliance of the overexposed flashback sequence, most of the film looks grayish to glum, although, in fact, outdoor scenes in bright sunlight do occur, but tend to be overshadowed by indoor sequences, or outdoor ones in bad weather or in the evening. By this means, the Alma-Frost episode achieves the character of a paradigm, contrasting with the rest of the film, and also, retroactively, irradiating it. The transitions in time within the flashback itself emphasize the eerie luminosity: they are shots of the sun behind a shifting veil of semitransparent clouds. The rest of the film—the present—looks, I repeat, gloomier or grayer; except when the light is a cruel and revealing one, as at the interview with Sjuberg and during the final humiliation in the circus, which is meant to recall the other brightly lighted scene—the flashback.

A striking set of images compares men and beasts. Most obvious is the parallel between the down-at-heel, adipose Albert and the decrepit, emaciated bear that Albert shoots just as he shot his own mirror image. There is an equally suggestive, though only momentary, equation of Anne's fear when Albert starts waving about the gun with the intensive fear and anger of Anne's black-and-white cat. The cat's very coloring suggests a relationship to the dark-haired and white-powdered Anne, herself a thoroughly feline creature. How Bergman got such an intense reaction from the cat (its ears seem to disappear into its nape), I cannot say; it

Albert, ringmaster.

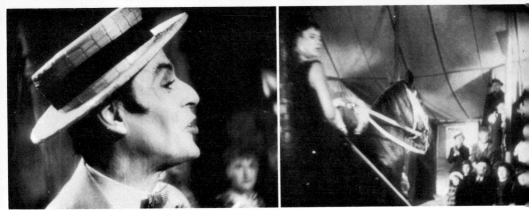

*Albert is goaded by Frans as Anne, a "Spanish Lady,"
rides around the ring.*

is one of the finest examples of animal emotion I have seen on film, and it is made particularly meaningful by being a combination of active wrath and passive fear. Such mixed emotions, canceling each other out and resulting in paralysis, characterize Anne's behavior, as well as that of various Bergman characters, in both this and other films.

No less apparent and suggestive is the comparison between Albert and a bull. Anne's faithlessness puts the finishing touch on him: a pair of horns. Earlier, when Anne was trying on costumes in the theatre attic, Blom, the janitor, playfully came at her in a bull's mask he had put on. It is not exactly a symbol, but there is something ominous about it. Soon afterward, Anne has occasion to rebuke Frans for rushing at her "blowing like a maddened bull," and we begin to wonder whether woman does not, in fact, turn all men into bulls. During his drinking session with Albert, Frost alludes to the great forthcoming circus performance "with horn music for horned cattle," and makes an accompanying gesture of fingers raised to the forehead. As Cowie writes, "One cannot help feeling that [*The Clown's Evening*] is directed from the standpoint of a matador, with Albert as the bull. He repeatedly staggers toward the camera until his puffed face is seen in gigantic proximity. Anne, Frans, Agda: all taunt him in different ways. Like a bull, he can only charge; he lacks any capacity for rational thought, and his stupidity is symbolized in the clumsy resistance he tenders to Frans in the ring. And if, at the very *mise-à-mort,* Albert is not dispatched, then his animal counterpart, the bear, *is.*" Unlike the bull, however, Albert may learn something from his various defeats; in-

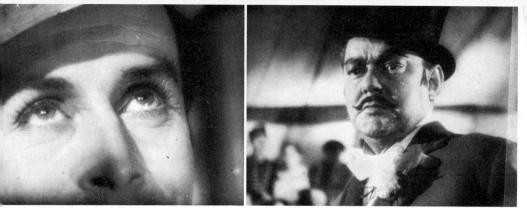

deed, under the influence of alcohol, he does confess a strange love-hate for Anne, and a sodden love for all people, stemming in part from the softening effects of suffering.

An equally important parallel seems to exist between the performing monkeys of the street organist who appears during the opening and closing credits (of the Swedish, though not the American, version). The monkeys perform both outside Agda's shop, where Albert suffers rejection, and outside Frans's dressing room, where Anne is used and swindled. These performing monkeys whose earnings go into the organ-grinder's pocket are not only the image of people being made monkeys of in their sexual affairs, but also the emblems of the actor and, even more, the circus artiste, whose monkeyshines earn them scant rewards. These parallels between men and animals reduce life in *The Clown's Evening* to a bestial simplicity, a coarseness that, nonetheless, is not without its pathos.

The contrast between stage and circus is one of the main strands of the film, with the superiority of the stage artist to the circus artiste emphasized, but with a dash of bitter irony. True, when Anne sees Frans committing stage suicide, she gives a little shriek: the artist's illusion is more sophisticated than the artiste's stunts, and the fact that Frans's illusion is mistaken by Anne for reality implies his superiority to her; the amulet of illusory value with which he cons her into giving him the reality of her body reaffirms that superiority. Finally, the easy victory of Frans over Albert, especially as won by a much smaller man by means of superior technique, seems to clinch the notion of theatrical intelligence and skill tri-

*Someone throws something into the ring. Anne's
horse rears, and she falls, a fallen woman. See
Frost's story, page 55.*

umphing over circus brute force and side-show exhibitionism. But
on closer examination, the theatre is shown as being of doubtful
superiority, as Sjuberg says in his big speech, for which Gunnar
Björnstrand uses an appropriately artificial, theatrical delivery.
The fake dagger with which Frans commits suicide while rehearsing a play aptly called *Betrayal* is the cousin of the worthless bau-
ble with which he treasonously conquers Anne. And his triumph
over Albert is, in part at least, accomplished by dirty fighting, by
kicking sawdust into his opponent's eyes—which is, again, related
to that spurious theatrical magic that consists of blinding one's
audience with illusions that, more often than not, turn to dust.

I have already alluded to the importance of mirrors in the film.
On the simplest level, this permits us to see the narcissism of the
actor or circus performer or plain human being in its most naked
form. Anne's greed for Frans's trinket, her almost indecent delight
in Sjuberg's costumes, become crystal-clear in the duplication and
solidification of the image in the looking glass. But Cowie is also
right when he observes that "the mirrors in the theatre obviate the
need for conventional cross-cutting and add a density to the
image, a look of abnormality." Already in *Summerplay* Bergman
had made extraordinary use of make-up mirrors in the ballerinas'
dressing room. The mirrors there, side by side but facing in opposite directions, created one of the fundamental Bergmanian mirror
effects: the change or estrangement of the shape and size of the
space in which people move. Thus just after we have seen the
caravans of *The Clown's Evening* in long shot at the film's beginning, we see them reflected in a river, from which view the camera

92

tilts upward to show the actual caravans crossing a bridge. The confusion of reality with its own reflection, Cowie calls this. So mirrors can confirm the illusory, or confound reality with delusion. In any case, a world in which mirrors preponderate is romantic, histrionic, neurotic, unreal. Over against this, Bergman posits the reality of suffering.

For it is through their own humiliations that Albert and Anne learn to commiserate with each other's. We live in a world of sham: the illusions of the theatre, the tricks of the circus merely echo the deceptions and self-deceptions of life. The already aging Alma trying to reassert her youth by symbolically copulating with an entire regiment, only to become an object of all-round ridicule, is emblematic of life's mockery that turns us all into clowns; the deadly repetitiousness of the traveling circus, symbolized by the way in which the closing shots reiterate the opening ones, is hardly different from the circular motion of the organ-grinder's hand squeezing out the monotonous tune to which monkeys and men perform. The only thing that can break the round of recurrent humiliations and defeats on the way to extinction is the little warmth we can proffer one another.

Thus Agda may be hopelessly petty-bourgeois and even smug, but she does sew on that button for Albert, a minuscule but real comfort. And there is something both more foolish and finer than Agda's sobriety and frugality about Albert's giving his last coin to his small son to spend on the organ-grinder and his monkeys. When Albert, as ringmaster, wants to cut the jeering Frans down to size, he does so by twice knocking the jaunty straw hat off the

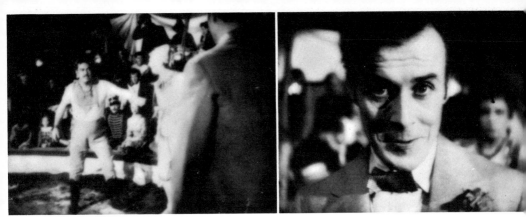

The fight between Albert and Frans—a series of
fast cuts.

actor's head with adroit cracks of his whip. Such a gesture, though mundanely naturalistic, is also symbolic and humane: the snottily superior Frans is forced to take his hat off to the "lady" he has abused. And though Frans, by his brutal tumbling of Albert in the sawdust (comparable to his tumbling into bed with Anne), gains the jubilation of the bestial crowd—into which Bergman ingeniously reintroduces the soldiery from Alma's and Frost's humiliation scene—and the admiring laughter of a brazen little actress, what will that avail him?

By contrast, Anne and Albert, through the solidarity they have shown for each other, are brought closer together in what may be a significant way. It is a powerful image, that medium shot of Anne, her face full of trepidation, awaiting Albert; then, after an exchange of minimal smiles, silently going on with him. After all these violent and wordy outbursts, what else is possible except silence and deeds? There is wonderfully acute observation in this, and I am dumbfounded when I read a serious critic like Vernon Young writing: "Bergman can invent; he can't observe." Or, for sheer accurate observation, consider the scene where Albert, after shooting the bear, seeks comfort in the stables. To quote the screen play: "The animals have a good acrid smell. Albert goes to the far end of the stall of the big black percheron named Prince. There his grief erupts in white flames, like a prairie fire. His head against the horse's neck, Albert Johansson weeps out all his drunkenness, and in the warmth of chagrin there commingle the humiliations, the fatigue, the despair, loneliness, disappointment, fear. . . . Finally, he sits on the ground, still weeping, and wipes his eyes and

94

Albert's humiliation. (See pages 56 and 57.)

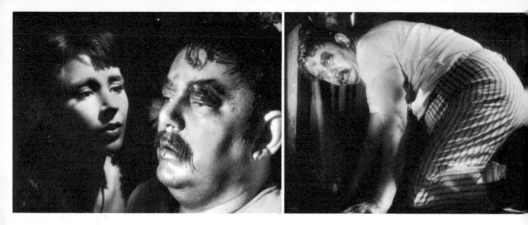

The humiliation has brought Anne and Albert
together. Bergman draws an obvious parallel: Albert
and the bear, whom he later shoots.
The curious and concerned circus folk wait outside
Albert's caravan, where he has gone to shoot himself.

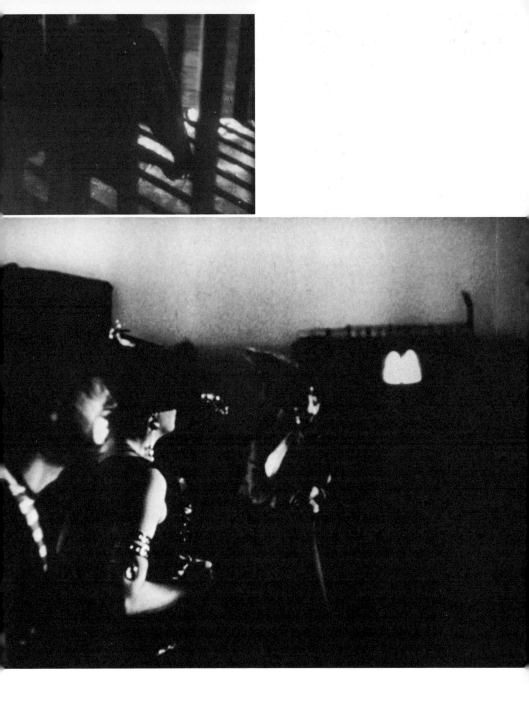

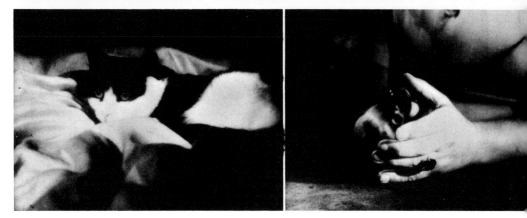

*Throughout the film, Bergman shows the human
animal by showing him among animals. Here, Anne's
cat reacts in fear as Albert tries to kill himself. He
cannot. He frees himself by shooting his image in
the mirror. Then he goes out and shoots the old bear
whom he so greatly resembles.*

nose with a handkerchief." In this closeness to the beasts, their
animal odors and warmth, which is the basic form of creature
comfort, man recognizes his essential nature, gathers himself together, and regains his ability to carry on.

Blomdahl's score, though somewhat reminiscent of Prokofiev and
perhaps also of the waltz scene from Alban Berg's *Wozzeck,* is a
paragon of sparing yet various use of music in film, and the performing of the cast is flawless. The late Åke Grönberg was an expert at portraying heavy but essentially jovial brutes such as the
sculptor Carl-Adam in *A Lesson in Love* and Albert Johansson in
this film. He was a man of thoroughly unprepossessing aspect, yet
it was a measure of his ability that he could convey the man under
the bear, and elicit our sympathy without in any way unduly playing upon it. Harriet Andersson's Anne is one of those remarkable
performances that the members of Bergman's repertory company
carry off with the most consummate bravura and the greatest, almost insolent, ease. Here she plays a voluptuous yet slightly infantile young woman: her face a mixture of provocation and naïveté,
her breasts heavy, her manner sensuous and teasing. She had just
played the heroine of *A Summer with Monika,* a slatternly, somewhat sullen, intensely physical teen-ager; her next role, after Anne,
was to be Nix, the tomboy daughter in *A Lesson in Love,* flat-
chested, afraid of sex, resentful of her parents' marital difficulties.

These are three very different parts, in which the actress carries off the most astonishing physical, to say nothing of psychic, transformations, only partly achieved by make-up and costuming. In the small part of Sjuberg, there is a highly finished performance by the man who was to become not only one of the great Bergmanian male principals, but also, in my opinion, one of the finest film actors of all time, Gunnar Björnstrand. Two other supporting performers, Gudrun Brost, as Alma, and Annika Tretow, as Agda, are likewise noteworthy.

But special mention must be made here of two extraordinary performances by actors who are not Bergman regulars. There is the Frans of Hasse Ekman, a role in which this extremely intelligent actor (also playwright and director) is given a much better chance than in such peripheral parts as the film director in *Prison* or the psychoanalyst in *Thirst.* Ekman's Frans is handsome, seemingly passionate, faintly effeminate, exaggeratedly virile, boyish, and cynical, with an almost ineffaceable sarcasm lodged in the corners of his eyes and mouth. One believes him to be capable of every kind of meanness—indeed, sees him practicing several choice varieties—yet he never loses a quintessential charm, and occasionally even suggests a true damned soul under his *beauté du diable.* A provincial Don Juan, a second-rate Byronic hero, this Frans seems to go through a life of paltry conquests unscathed and smiling. And though those scratches Anne engraves on his face doubtless leave no permanent scar, we are inclined to wonder whether this actor whom we watch rehearsing such an impassioned, even if bogus, suicide scene, whose first wooing of Anne appears to be truly desperate and paroxysmal, is only the petty seducer one would dismiss him as?

Even more extraordinary is the Frost of Anders Ek, an actor of slightly above average height who actually manages to look very tall and gangly in the film. In his clown's make-up, he succeeds in being comic and pathetic, so brilliantly both at once that we lose the distinction—exactly as the film wants us to. When Albert's gun is aimed at his temple, Frost's face achieves an expression that is the height of the tragicomic; in the flashback, he permits the pathos to preponderate; in other scenes, he maintains a wonderful dignity underneath the surface clowning. Ek uses a southern, quasi-Danish accent for Frost, which gives him the kind of yokelishness Yankees associate with some of our Southern accents. When in the last scene we see Frost out of make-up for the first time (another

Till at last I was just a little seed, and then I vanished.

The journey continues . . .

Bergman master stroke), his recounting of his dream assumes added gravity, and Ek's voice itself emerges from its clown's garb to deliver these lines with a heightened poetic and philosophic charge. It is a performance of great variety within a relatively narrow scope. How regrettable that the actor has appeared to date in only two other Bergman works: *The Seventh Seal,* where he excelled in the brief part of the flagellant monk, and in *The Ritual,* a rather unsatisfactory chamber film made for television, in which, however, Ek does very well in a contemporary role.

What is the final impact of *The Clown's Evening?* What world view does it convey? The answer is contained in these lines of the screenplay, much shortened in the film, presumably to make its "message" less conspicuous. In the scenario, the drunken Albert maunders: "Poor Anne! Poor Agda! Poor me! Poor little boys! And you, you moron, and your poor wife! Poor all of us, all men who live on earth, and who are, all of us, so scared, so scared, so scared!" This may well be the master theme of Bergman's *oeuvre,* and it is to the credit of this early film to have given it such sovereign expression.

for Anne and Albert.

104

SMILES OF A
SUMMER NIGHT

This is the life —

ere s no

The two films following *The Clown's Evening* strike me as the two most underrated minor gems in Bergman's catalogue. *A Lesson in Love* (1954) is a delicious comedy with serious overtones about conjugal difficulties, the generation gap, and changing concepts of love and marriage, which ends with the reassertion of marital fidelity as the best, although arduous, solution. There is great range here, from subtle comedy to roisterous farce, and the acting and directing are as smooth as elegance can get without turning into superficiality. Also in a contemporary setting, but this time looking at marriage and the family from the outside, from the point of view of those who might break them up, is *Women's Dreams* (1955; released here as *Dreams*), a drama with occasional comic overtones. It is a serious, moving, maturely humane film, and, like *A Lesson in Love,* suffers only from comparison with other, even better, films by its maker. If in the earlier film the plight of a daughter whose parents are splitting up was particularly affecting, here we are gripped by the trials of the long-suffering mistress of a man who won't divorce his wife, and by the fiasco of a rich, unhappy older man who vainly seeks the balm of love from a flighty young girl.

These, granted, are stock situations, as are those of *Smiles of a Summer Night* (1955), Bergman's comic masterpiece to date. But the way in which these traditional comic plots are accumulated, intertwined, and resolved is highly original and absolutely masterly. Fredrik Egerman, a middle-aged roué of a lawyer, has a very

All photographs in this chapter courtesy Janus Films.

young second wife, Anne, with whom he has not yet consummated his two-year-old marriage. He also has a young son, Henrik, a brilliant theological student, confused and repressed, secretly in love with Anne, and trying to have an affair with the willing Petra, Anne's young maid, but unable to have successful intercourse without love. Fredrik takes Anne to see the great actress Desirée Armfeldt in a play, and Anne, who has guessed that Desirée was formerly Fredrik's mistress, breaks into tears and asks to be taken home soon after the play begins. Fredrik later returns to the theatre alone, has a merry time reminiscing with Desirée and her old dresser, Malla, and accepts an invitation to the actress's apartment. On the way, he falls into a puddle and has to change into a nightshirt and bathrobe belonging to Count Carl-Magnus Malcolm, Desirée's current lover, who arrives unexpectedly on a short leave from army maneuvers. Malcolm, a dangerous womanizer and fierce duelist, ejects Egerman in his nightshirt.

Desirée, who wants Fredrik to marry her, gets her rich, eccentric old mother to invite a few people to a house party in her country home at Ryarp. Count Malcolm arrives with his bitter young wife, Charlotte, who hates him for his infidelities yet also adores him. Fredrik comes with Anne, who is eager to examine her experienced rival, Desirée, at close range; and with Henrik, now lost in love for his girl-stepmother, a love that she, unbeknown to herself, reciprocates. With them is Petra, who promptly starts dallying with Frid, the old lady's coachman, a strong, lusty, devil-may-care fellow in the prime of life. Desirée and Charlotte form an alliance to effectuate a scheme of the actress's whereby the actress will get Fredrik for herself and the Countess will regain full possession of her husband. At dinner, Desirée and Charlotte taunt Malcolm into betting his wife that she could not seduce Egerman in fifteen minutes. All the glib talk about seduction makes Henrik burst out with horror and hurt, but Anne so lovingly, so sovereignly calms him down that Fredrik, with a pang, perceives that the two young people are in love. But Henrik has another outburst and rushes into the garden; Anne, terrified that he might do himself some injury, tearfully withdraws to bed.

Charlotte begins to seduce the anguished Fredrik as the rest of the group go off to the yellow pavilion, to hear Desirée sing a German *lied* on the *carpe diem* theme. Meanwhile Henrik tries to hang himself in his bedroom, but the cord slips and he falls against a knob that was installed in this room years ago for the King: it

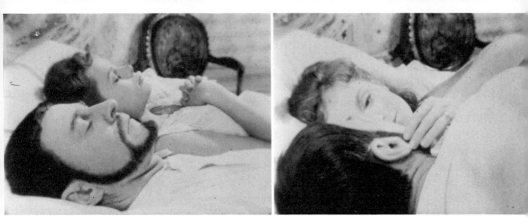

*Theatrical structure: all combinations of relation-
ships are treated in terms of "scenes" with strongly
delineated characters.
The first duet, Fredrik Egerman and Anne. Egerman
says the wrong name . . .*

makes a bed from the adjoining bedroom, in which the King's mistress, the wife of one of his ministers, used to sleep, glide in
through the wall. The bed now moves in with the sleeping Anne in
it. Henrik and Anne declare their love for each other and enlist the
help of Petra and Frid, who have been making love in the shed;
the maid and groom get a carriage ready for the lovers to elope in.
Egerman, from the shadows, watches them drive off; suffering silently, he heads for a tryst in the pavilion with Charlotte, who, apparently, is ready to double-cross Desirée and follow through on
her conquest. The actress espies them from a window and alerts
Count Malcolm; the enraged husband shows up in the pavilion
with a pistol.

The women wait anxiously outside while Malcolm obliges Fredrik to play Russian roulette with him. The gun goes off against the
lawyer's temple, but the bullet is a blank filled with soot. Desirée
lovingly washes Fredrik and puts him to bed; he will marry her and
legitimize her little son, Fredrik, Jr., whom the lawyer did not even
know he had fathered. Malcolm, having lost the bet, pays up: he
will be faithful to his wife—in his fashion. Petra extracts a promise
of marriage from Frid, who has a streak of the poet in him and expatiates on the three smiles of the summer night (*i.e.,* the three
phases of oncoming dawn): for young lovers, for contented fools,
and for the wretched of this world.

In such condensation, the plot does not begin to suggest the

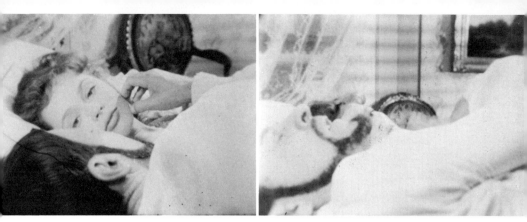

brilliance of the film. But, even from this précis, the clever geometrical construction is apparent. Henrik oscillates between Petra and Anne, Anne between Henrik and Fredrik. Fredrik fluctuates between Anne and Desirée, Desirée between Fredrik and Malcolm, Malcolm between Desirée and Charlotte, and Charlotte between Malcolm and Fredrik. We have come full circle. On the lower social level, Petra similarly swings between Henrik and Frid, and Frid between Petra and his bachelorhood and freedom. Only old Mrs. Armfeldt on the upper level (like Malla, the dresser, on the lower) is above it all, surveying the whirligig with dispassionate amusement and a grain of malice. But she, too, when young and not above the fray, was buffeted between one lover and another. *Smiles of a Summer Night* is constructed like one of those elaborate molecules in which atoms rearrange themselves in the heat of emotions and under the stress of circumstances. In a sense, the ending of the film is an isomer of its beginning. This quasi-mathematical, or even biochemical, structure of the film might suggest schematism; but such is the genius of the controlling artist that the mechanistic skeleton puts on flesh and that, in turn, becomes instinct with spirit. Starting from the fact that Egerman in one instance hums a snatch of Mozart, Robin Wood has evolved an elaborate parallel between *Smiles* and Mozartian opera. This is given some corroboration by Bergman's avowed love of Mozart (and use of him in *Hour of the Wolf*); and Wood's juxtaposition is both illuminating and suggestive. To me, however, the film begs even more for comparison with three art forms: theatre, dance, and music.

Theatricality permeates *Smiles of a Summer Night* as meaningfully as thoroughly. Most obviously, Desirée Armfeldt is a distinguished actress, and she sets the stage for that Midsummer Night's

"Desirée!"

house party (in the area of Skåne, the scene also of *The Clown's Evening*) that turns, quite literally, into bedroom farce; she is both one of the principal players in and the director of that aestival entertainment. More significantly, the plays within the film set the tone for its action. The countess whom Desirée portrays in the comedy Fredrik and Anne are watching verbalizes and embodies the philosophy of the film: that women, by skillful manipulation, control the destinies of men. These self-effacing puppeteers allow their marionettes not only an illusion of complete independence but even delusions of undisputed superiority. Again, near the end of the film, when Desirée is about to become Egerman's wife-mother, replacing his escaped child-wife, she rehearses another play in which her lines express her situation: woman, aging and becoming the prey of loneliness and anxiety, wants to be the wife of a suitable man, not just his fleeting diversion.

But the most striking way in which the film resembles theatre is in its emphasis on brilliant dialogue, on people confronting one another in enclosed spaces, on bringing action and reaction into the same frame. People doing something and someone else observing them become part of the same image or are shown in rapid succession, reproducing or simulating the simultaneous interaction that is the specialty of the stage. Most, if not all, of the scenes of *Smiles* could be translated without much difficulty onto a spacious and well-equipped stage, and I know of at least one time when the screen play was actually performed as a play. Now this theatricality of the film is not just a whim; still less is it a limitation of Bergman's. The purpose is to show the theatricality of life: life as a sequence of scenes from a comedy, sometimes verging on tragedy, occasionally lapsing into farce. From this comparison, another one follows: that of people to actors. And, indeed, everyone in the film is acting at least one part (*e.g.,* the Count as Don Juan) or several (Desirée as woman of the world with the Count, great actress yet also warm lover with Fredrik, dutiful daughter with old Mrs. Armfeldt, and "just one of us women" with Charlotte). Even the innocents are acting: Anne pretends to be more adult, more housewifely than she is; Henrik pretends to greater religious dedication than he actually possesses.

This theatricality and play-acting suggest the disguises, the unreality, the brittleness of life as Bergman sees it—or, at least, sees it here. The lovely costumes into and out of which the women are often seen changing, the elegant period décor (1901, according to the script), a certain dwelling of the camera on luxuries of various kinds contribute to the sense of dressing up, wearing masks, playing roles. But these highly theatrical scenes are nevertheless also cinematic, as I suggested in *Private Screenings:* "For example, the almost unbearably ornate crystal goblets [I should have added: chandelier, silverware, jewelry], by their aspect and their positioning in the image, convey the oppressive luxuriousness of the diners' lives in purely and uniquely filmic terms. Composition, lighting, photographic texture, editing translate a scene into cinematic idiom so perfectly that it matters little whether it was originally conceived in theatrical . . . terms." The final effect of all this theatricality is to convey the unreality of reality.

And surely many things in *Smiles of a Summer Night* could happen only in a play, where events are controlled by the playwright. Why else should Henrik accidentally hit the knob that brings the sleeping Anne to him through the wall; why should she even have, unwittingly, picked the right bed? Why, when Carl-Magnus and Fredrik play Russian roulette, should the soot-filled blank go off only on the last try, prolonging the lawyer's agony and the filmgoer's suspense? And why shouldn't it have gone off at the Count's temple? And why should the Count, who says one doesn't risk one's life with a shyster, be willing to risk humiliation with such a one? Do comic-dramatic accidents like these happen in life or only in drama? It is the film's achievement that you both disbelieve and believe them: no, this is only a play; but yes, life *is* a play, a game, a series of accidents so unlikely as to seem rigged. The essence of this duality is captured in a short exchange between Fredrik and Charlotte during their tryst in the yellow pavilion. "*Fredrik:* Are you really real, by the way? *Charlotte:* Haven't you noticed that I am a character in a play, that we are playing a

Backstage: Fredrik, who has returned to Desirée in
his dreams, now physically enacts his return, winding
his way to her through a maze of doors and curtains.
Theatre melds with life. (*See* The Clown's Evening.)

ridiculous farce? *Fredrik:* Yes, that's true. *Charlotte:* We're de-
ceived, we're betrayed, we're deserted. We are *really* ridiculous."
Notice how all this hinges on words like "real," "really," and "true"
—but what is real and true is the comedy, the play-acting, the unreality of it all. And the fact that it is hard to tell whether Charlotte
would really have gone through with the seduction of Fredrik (as
Desirée's reaction implies) or wouldn't have (as her passion for
her husband suggests), and that the tête-à-tête is soon interrupted,
anyhow, merely adds to the sense of dislocation and unreality.

But *Smiles of a Summer Night* is perhaps even more like a dance
than like a play, one of those old-fashioned dances in which one
keeps changing partners but ends with the one whose dance it is.
For much as the characters waltz back and forth between likely
and unlikely partners, they all end up where they really belong—
though that does not necessarily mean a wholly happy ending.
The civilized yet in many ways immature lawyer Egerman, who for
all his visions of himself as a dominant personality needs a mature
woman to look after him, gets one in Desirée; just as she, sensible
of impending age and the need to retire from the theatre, gets a
suitably affluent man whom she really likes and can nicely control.
Anne, young and innocent, wedded in name only to Fredrik, ends
up with Henrik, pure and idealistic, and likewise wedded to the
church in name only. The Count and Countess are temporarily reunited on terms that are at least superficially hopeful, though as
the Count gives his wife the kiss of reconciliation and promise of

when the old billy-goat turns tender-hearted celibate.

relative fidelity, his hand that clasps Charlotte's head still holds the pistol, and the suggestion of an armed truce, an unstable peace, is beautifully conveyed. Still, Carl-Magnus and Charlotte, grim fighters both, haters as much as lovers, are perfectly matched. So, too, are Frid and Petra: tough, shrewd, sensual, and earthy.

A dance, then—a quadrille or minuet—that subsumes numerous little dances or dancelike movements: the provocative, hip-swinging walk with which Petra drives Henrik wild; Anne waltzing around with the dress she proposes to wear to the theatre; Egerman and Malla following the singing and swaying Desirée home from the theatre; Petra and Anne rolling around Anne's bed in an access of wild laughter and youthful exuberance; old and invalid Mrs. Armfeldt being carried hither and yon in Frid's arms; Frid, barefoot and with satyrlike leaps, chasing Petra into the summer night; and Petra, barefoot in turn, racing back to the kitchen as the film ends, with the contentedly captured Frid trotting after her. And, most significant of all, there is the round of figures on the tower clock, twice shown circling around at the stroke of the hour; among them glides the last dancer, Death.

Moreover, Bergman has meticulously choreographed the movements of his actors. Take the scene in which the guests at Ryarp exchange extremely formal greetings on the front lawn as they eye potential adversaries or allies. Or take the moment after, when Desirée shows Charlotte to her room, and the two women pass on either side of the Count to converge behind his back, where, figuratively, they will scheme to get him reunited with his wife. Or, again, the night escapade of Petra and Frid: the chases, the tumbling in the hay, Frid's movements mirroring those of the windmill while the sound track is ecstatically awash with bird song, horses' neighing, and the ringing of distant bells. And consider so simple

Egerman and Desirée, another duet.

and shocking a piece of choreography as the one that occurs after Henrik has darted out into the night, and the tearful and worried Anne has asked Fredrik's permission to retire: Egerman stands dazed and hurt, aware of the truth at last, and as Petra rushes to her mistress and sweeps upstairs with her, the two pass behind the lawyer's back and slightly bump him as they move away. There is something brilliantly conceived about that bumping: it manages to epitomize Fredrik's downfall, the end of his control over Anne, Henrik, the situation, life itself. The dance goes on without his calling the tune any longer.

The analogy between the film and music is also of paramount importance. Bergman, as we know, loves music, and in many of his films it plays an important dramatic part. In *Smiles,* however, it is the film as a whole that aspires to the condition of music. Most obviously, there is the music-box tune that seems to emerge from a little cherub's trumpet and coyly heralds the coming of that trick bed through the wall. Thus music accompanies the supreme romantic fulfillment in the film. But music also celebrates love in general, as in Desirée's song when she leads her little procession through the nocturnal streets. And music, again, utters the primal warning, "Seize the day!" when Desirée, accompanying herself on the harp, gives her recital in the yellow pavilion. That harp later looms between the heads of Fredrik and Charlotte during their amorous skirmishing, and presides also over the ensuing game of Russian roulette, suggesting that harmony will yet come out of these embroilments. During their confrontation in Desirée's sitting room, while embarrassedly awaiting the actress's return, Malcolm whistles a march, and Fredrik promptly retaliates by humming a snatch of Mozart; each defines his outlook musically. Music figures even in meaningful travesty, as when the cuckoo on Desirée's

117

clock announces the hour, and both the Count and the lawyer feel that they are being cuckolded. Or consider the martial noises with which Malcolm's automobile pulls up before the Armfeldt mansion: a whole comic sequence of puffs and sputters ending with a fierce but foolish bang.

The score by Erik Nordgren is truly minimal, a discreet, sporadic musical underscoring, featuring one lovely but carefully underused melody. To be sure, there are the two loud clashes of cymbals (or something like it)—signifying jealousy, agony, a terrible awakening—first at the dinner table, when Fredrik becomes aware of his wife's and son's love for each other; and, later, when he watches from the shadows as the two young people elope. These may be unsubtle; but how marvelously music and images blend in a device Bergman uses to mark the passage of time during Midsummer Night. This is a sequence of three shots: (1) the moon, with clouds drifting before it, (2) swans gliding across a pond, (3) a long shot looking toward the lovely neo-classic mansion bathed in moonlight and reflected in the basin of a fountain. This sequence is twice repeated for purposes of transition, and is accompanied on the sound track by the chirping of birds and three harp arpeggios acting, as it were, as an auditory wipe. The three images— moon, swans, house—are themselves like exquisite, floating arpeggios, bridges between the stanzas of a song; and the harp points toward Desirée's *lied,* whose German words admonish: "Rejoice in life while the little lamp yet glows! Before it has withered, gather the rose. . . ." It is into the sweetly melancholy words and melody of this song that the entire film, in the end, seems to dissolve.

What the film does with great skill and finesse is to examine the entire spectrum of attitudes toward love as they vary according to age and social status. Bergman has created archetypal figures that are nevertheless not lacking in specific individuality, and that, among them, supply a compendium, a veritable lexicon of wisdom and folly about love. As a result, it is almost impossible for any viewer not to indentify himself or herself with one or more persons in the film. Take, for example, the wonderfully rich character of Fredrik Egerman, prototype of the mellow, rather cynical, sophisticated yet also secretly vulnerable upper-middle-class lover. His attitudes are defined to a large extent by his easygoing, peaceable, unheroic, comfortably bourgeois background and financial well-being; and they are further shaped by his having reached the

118

*The "scene"—"man to man"
Enter Malcolm.*

Malcolm shows his "prowess." He throws a knife . . .

age (and, with it, the degree of experience) that enables him to look back upon considerable sensory satisfactions, and forward to a still goodly supply of amatory years. It is thus that he can contemplate his former mistress in her bathtub—Desirée, who is at the same stage of ripeness and sophistication as he, but, being a shrewd woman as well, free of Fredrik's childishly sentimental self-indulgence—and say these words in answer to her question whether he finds her still as beautiful as then: "You are as beautiful and as desirable. The years have given your body the perfection that perfection itself lacks, an excitement that perfection does not have." This, as we look at Gunnar Björnstrand delivering the line, and imagine the naked body of Eva Dahlbeck (tactfully left to our imagination—indeed, Fredrik himself utters his encomium with his eyes closed!), strikes us as much more than elegant gallantry. We are in the fully dramatized, naked presence of a great truth about love.

But this same Fredrik Egerman must resort to being avuncular with his untouched child bride; defensively sardonic with his son, the strength of whose youth he secretly fears; and cautiously generous to Petra, whose sensuality he savors but cannot afford to get entangled with. Toward Count Malcolm, a stronger but less witty rival, he is pointedly ironic; under different circumstances, if he were not so badly hurt by Anne and Henrik, he would be quite a match for Charlotte, too. He is, in short, a man of many sides in his emotional and erotic commerce, succinctly and evocatively delineated from all of them. And we see him also divested of all his defenses, perplexed by his wife's changing moods, beginning to doubt that he will ever truly possess her: "When he has returned

120

at a woman's portrait—then coolly bites into an apple.
Exit Fredrik.

123

Desirée journeys to see her mother. (See pages 14 and 15.)

to his study, he sits down at the table, smokes for a few minutes while he looks thoughtfully out of the window. Then he takes out his wallet and extracts Anne's photographs. He places them in a row on the table before him, leans forward, touches them one after another with his forefinger. His eyeglasses cloud up. He has to take them off and wipe them with his handkerchief. He holds them up to the light. His face is intense and the membranes of his eyes feel brittle with suppressed sorrow." How graphically, how visually this is conceived: the man who does not dare to possess the real girl by his side—his legal wife, who actually gives him certain encouragements he manages to miss—but who wistfully, achingly fingers her photographs. These photographs, incidentally, sum up the Fredrik-Anne relationship: the first time he sees them, his attitude is proud and possessive; the second time—this—he already uses them as a substitute for reality; the last time, in the pavilion after the Russian roulette duel, he bids them, as it were, farewell. Desirée, tough but humane, pockets them. She does not tear them up; she merely puts them aside as a toy Fredrik must realize he has outgrown: the dream of Anne is swallowed up by the reality of Desirée.

Now consider the scene between Desirée and her mother. Everything about and around the little old lady is white or at least pale; only Desirée, in what I like to think is a red dress and a matching hat, photographs very black indeed, and stands out in intense, passionate contrast with her surroundings. The old lady represents a superiority to love based on superannuation ("bodily decrepitude is wisdom," says Yeats, not without bitter irony); she represents the detachment of an experienced but no longer involved onlooker, now living only to pamper herself with creature comforts. She sighs, "You can never protect a single human being

from suffering. That's what makes one so horribly tired." In a sense, this is self-delusion: you justify your not being able to love any more by invoking the futility of trying to help, protect, love anyone in this life, thus making of physiological debility a metaphysical principle. But, in another sense, there is a great deal of truth in the statement, and one wonders whether any of the lovers in the film, once Midsummer Night is over, will be able to protect his partner's and his own happiness. Significantly, the old lady plays solitaire, looks tiny in her overlarge bed, and is surrounded by pallor and whiteness: visual devices that suggest her elimination, both placid and wistful, from the game of love. She has to admit: "I am tired of people, but it doesn't stop me from loving them."

Old Mrs. Armfeldt's remark points toward a curious, paradoxical aspect of this film: that most of its lovers, much as they chase after love, really dread and decry it. When Henrik sarcastically asks his father whether he claims that young men cannot love, Fredrik answers, "Yes, of course. A young man always loves himself, loves his self-love, and his love of love itself." Whereupon the following exchange takes place. "*Henrik* (ironic): But at your mature age, of course, one knows what it means to love. *Fredrik:* I think so. *Henrik* (ironic): That must be wonderful. *Fredrik:* It's terrible, my son, and one doesn't know how to stand it. *Henrik:* Are you being sincere now, Father?" From the small, unhappy smile with which Fredrik responds, one assumes that he does mean it—mean it as much as these complacently buffeted people can mean anything.

And so, again, when Frid and Petra are having their sex and beer in the hay. As Frid unexpectedly proves to have a touch of the poet about him while he talks of the first smile of the summer night being for young lovers, Petra sadly wonders, "Why have I never

"Woman to woman." As Desirée confronts her mother and hears her memories, she sees herself. (See pages 66 and 67 for a different use of the mirror.)

been a young lover?" The coachman tells her not to feel sorry, for "There are only a very few young lovers on this earth. You can almost count them on your fingers. Love has smitten them both as a gift and as a punishment." As for the others, "We invoke love, cry out for it, beg for it; we play the game, we think we've got it, and lie about it." But, in the end, Frid and Petra seem quite content not to have the gift of young love—or the punishment.

Perhaps the most passionate person among the dramatis personae is Charlotte Malcolm, yet even she has her outburst against men (*i.e.,* her husband) and love (*i.e.,* her husband): "Men are beastly! They are silly and vain and have hair all over their bodies." After which she weeps and adds in a low voice, "Love is a disgusting business." Lovers, true lovers, on the other hand, do not attack, disparage, or even reckon the pluses and minuses of love: they simply live it. And so when Anne and Henrik end up in each other's arms, the dialogue reaches a sort of Maeterlinckian, rather too stylized, innocence: "*Anne:* Henrik. *Henrik:* Anne. *Anne:* I love you. *Henrik:* I love you. *Anne:* I loved you from the very first. *Henrik:* I loved you from the very first." Happy families have no history, Tolstoy informs us; happy men have no shirts, Anatole France instructs us; happy lovers, we learn here, have no conversation.

But if love is a dubious proposition, if it so often misfires, if it is so rare and perishable, we have no one but ourselves to blame for it—ourselves and our social-butterfly existences. By a curious coincidence, the great poet Rainer Maria Rilke spent a summer and

126

fall in Skåne, staying at various country houses not unlike Ryarp, where the climax of *Smiles* takes place. The time was 1904, only three years after the supposed date of the film. In a letter to his wife, just a few days after Midsummer Night, Rilke tells her that he intends to stay in his little guest room and work: "For the downstairs rooms are large halls; in one of them one eats, the other is a sort of drawing room . . . in it, there is unrest, coming and going, and the lives of others are very close there." * It is in such a hall, or *Saal,* as Rilke calls it, that the key scene of *Smiles* unfolds, the dinner at which the crucial events to follow announce themselves. And indeed the lives of others there impinge on everyone's private or conjugal life. The saturnine looks of the servants, the elaborate but cold glitter of the setting, perfectly frame the animated façades of the diners from behind which intrigue darts forth in the form of badinage.

The wonder of this dinner scene lies in Bergman's seeing all sides of the problem. Henrik idealistically rebels against the cynicism of his elders who discuss the relations between the sexes in martial imagery; Malcolm constructs an extended, brutal metaphor, and Desirée sums it up succinctly, "Mature people treat love either as a military exploit or as a gymnastics display." Yet Henrik's innocent indignation has something intolerant and uncouth about it, so that old Mrs. Armfeldt can wonder with some justice: "Why is youth so terribly unmerciful? And who gave it permission to be that way?" To the conqueror male, Count Malcolm, Bergman counterposes Fredrik Egerman, the man who prefers to be seduced by women; alongside the canny Desirée, there is the headlong Charlotte. And there is Anne, who was childish with Fredrik, but

* Letter, June 26, 1904. In the original: ". . . *dort ist Unruhe, Kommen und Gehen, und das Leben der anderen ist dort ganz nahe.*"

127

Dinner at Mrs. Armfeldt's: all the characters are assembled for a full range of combinations on which all further action will turn. As the old lady speaks of the wine's mystic powers, we see each individual response and each character clearly defined. (See Winter Light, *the opening Communion scene, page 149.) Bergman often uses dinner scenes to accomplish dramatic ends, for example, in* Through a Glass Darkly, The Magician, Hour of the Wolf, A Passion.

The outcome of all the various combinations of relationships: Henrik and Anne; Fredrik and Desirée; Malcolm and Charlotte; Petra and Frid. Bergman heightens the actions and environment of each couple to express their characteristics. Frid: "There isn't a better life than this."

now, toward Henrik, becomes motherly. The way in which each diner responds to the old lady's toast, the words or attitudes with which each drains his or her glass of wine, beautifully epitomizes each personality, and with each—even with the conflicting aspects of each—Bergman is in compassionate sympathy.

Yet this sympathy does not exclude an ironic lucidity. Every character is perceived as twofold: what he visualizes himself as and what we recognize him to be. Egerman, the superior man of the world, is also an aging, slightly pathetic loser; Desirée, the self-sufficient actress ("I have the *theatre,* sir, and the theatre is my life . . ."), is also a lonely woman of uncertain age in need of a husband and father for her illegitimate son; Anne, who imagines herself to be an accomplished little housekeeper, is really helpless and useless around the house; and so on. Only the servants are essentially what they appear to be; Bergman's view of them is both nostalgic and patronizing, and reminds one of certain British dramatists of the recent past: James Barrie, Noel Coward, and even Bernard Shaw. If there are contradictions in the servants' make-up, they work in the possessor's favor; thus it is a strange, almost incredible, paradox to have the boisterously mundane Frid utter the film's most poetic, and eponymous, conceit; but it is also satisfying that he should have this poetry in him: it makes us feel better about

This is the life — here's no...

his getting Petra, for whom we would have otherwise entertained higher expectations.

The fundamental irony is located both in the characters and in something deeper yet: life itself. If Carl-Magnus is ruthless and domineering but cannot help it if women lead him by the nose, that is irony based in character. Henrik bids farewell to his virtue with a lovely and comic outcry: "O Lord, if your world is sinful, then I want to sin. Let the birds build nests in my hair; * take my miserable virtue from me, because I can't bear it any longer." This from a youth who is watching Frid and Petra head for their sexual frolic, and who, we assume, means to give himself over to carnality. But it is the irony of Henrik's nature that he can be neither a saint nor a sinner, and so the impulse to sex turns into attempted suicide. Thus far the irony of character; now, however, the irony of life itself takes over, and, by the wildest of accidents, dispatches Anne into the boy's arms. Whosoever cannot be either sinner or saint is —for that very reason, perhaps—cut out to be a lover.

It is such a metaphysical irony, too, that makes Fredrik mutter Desirée's name in his half-sleep, just at the moment when Anne is aroused enough to succumb to him—and the consummation of this marriage, of course, would have changed the futures of all the film's characters. And it is by such a superior, impersonal irony that, just as Desirée and Fredrik reach a stalemate about to send them on their separate ways forever, Carl-Magnus pops in—not to help part these former lovers but, ironically, to effect their ultimate

---

* The reference is to a passage from Luther, with which Henrik sermonizes both Anne and Petra: ". . . in discussing temptation, Martin Luther says: You cannot prevent the birds from flying over your head, but you can prevent them from nesting in your hair."

union. This cosmic irony, though, is not always a benevolent one. When Fredrik watches his wife and son rapturously drive off into the night, Anne's veil becomes undone and flutters to the ground not far from the lawyer. As the betrayed husband and father picks up the veil, a shot from the rear reveals him suddenly as an old man: his shoulders hunched, his back stiff as he awkwardly stoops to gather the wispy garment. A sad irony registers on us as surely as on him: the veil of Anna's virginity, which he was too scrupulous or weak to rend, is now his—but without the girl who wore it. He who contents himself with surfaces will get the surface and nothing beyond it. And, I suppose, there is something faintly sad, too, about the last shot of Desirée in the film as she sits on the steps outside the pavilion in which Fredrik is sleeping off his unhappy experiences. The actress is watching over the lawyer who is now hers. From her pocket, she takes the script she has been memorizing and a cigar on which she proceeds to puff pleasurably. Cigars were the emblems of Fredrik's comfortable paternalism; now the symbol of authority has shifted mouths.

There are many such exquisite details in the film, emblematizing a character or situation with a single gesture or image. Thus the ardent Charlotte makes her first entrance as a flame. Malcolm is in his bowling alley, which he has converted into a shooting gallery: he always turns innocuous games into deadly ones—thus he makes of croquet an exercise in sadism when, at Ryarp, he plays against Egerman. The script reads: "He takes out a cigarette and looks on the table for matches. Suddenly a flame flashes at the tip of his cigarette." Only in the next shot do we see Charlotte proffering the light. Most appropriate, for Charlotte is a small, intense, jealous flame pursuing her elusive husband. And, equally significant, as she and the Count start their malevolent banter (Stanley

Universal time—in which all dramas are set.

Kauffmann has called the film a comedy "more barbed than funny"), she takes a few practice shots at the target, and the angrier she becomes at her husband, the more deadly accurate her aim gets to be.

Or consider the cunning symbolism of man's capitulation before woman. When the singing Desirée leads Egerman to her apartment, there are beautiful shots of the tiny procession reflected in the puddles along the street; into one of these the lawyer falls, much to his ex-mistress's amusement. A little later, we learn from a somewhat begrimed Malcolm that, as he was riding toward Desirée, his horse stumbled and threw him. Observe what happens to these two very different men after their symbolic falls: the lawyer is reduced to becoming outfitted with his rival's nightshirt, cap, and robe, and ends up looking domesticated and ridiculous. The Count is undaunted by his fall: he hands Desirée an outlandish bouquet and declares solemnly: "Here are some simple flowers I managed to pick from a nearby garden. I didn't want to come empty-handed." Malcolm can convert even a fall into a triumph— he will appropriate alien flowers as casually as he will another man's woman—but there is something absurd and almost pitiful about such a victory.

In such a deliberately theatrical rather than cinematic film, visual bravura effects must of necessity be rare; they do, however, occur. There is, for example, something fascinating about the use windows are put to in the Ryarp scenes. It is through a window that Desirée and Charlotte, planning their strategy, watch Malcolm gloatingly knock Egerman's croquet ball out of bounds. Seeing the latter scene first in long shot emphasizes its smallness and remoteness from immediate reality: while the women pull the strings of destiny, the men are content to play, with utmost seriousness, ludicrous little competitive games. Again, it is through a window that the agonized Henrik watches, enviously and miserably, Frid and Petra engaging in a Priapic chase through the blessed summer night. The shot through the window, as before, introduces a change of camera angles and pace into the scene—throws it open, as it were—while sharply emphasizing the differences between the world of the onlooker and that of the people his gaze yearns toward. Later, it is through such a window again that Desirée sees Fredrik and Charlotte come together in the pavilion: a light goes up in the little pleasure dome as well as under Desirée's great domed forehead. The contrast is once more between the conscientious, perhaps too deliberately scheming, Desirée, and the lawyer and Countess, who are about to immerse themselves in a mere game. Later still, after the shot goes off inside the pavilion, the anxious women outside glimpse the pistol-carrying Count gliding past the windows and assume that he has just killed his rival. So much of our seeing seems to be done through windows, and always on one side or the other there is greater clarity of perception, surer knowledge at work—teasing, flouting, controlling the consciousness across the divide.

But probably the most telling image of the film is that of Anne dashing to her clothes closet in a fit of joy at being taken to the theatre, and not knowing which dress to wear. Finally, picking up one, she announces triumphantly: "Yes, I know! The white one! The white one is suitable for both laughter and tears." From the other room, Henrik and Fredrik are watching her. Henrik sadly, because he loves her and she is his father's wife; Fredrik happily, because he is fond and proud of her, and hopes truly to possess her. But soon Henrik will be rejoicing in Anne's love and running off with her, while Fredrik will be left tearfully behind. Such is the comedy, or tragicomedy, of life; such, perhaps, is the play to which Fredrik and Anne are going, of which neither of them is destined to see much; and such, certainly, is *Smiles of a Summer Night,* one of those true great comedies which, though very funny at times, are never far removed from tears. White, which, under different circumstances, can be the symbol of either rejoicing or mourning, is the right color for this film.

Many, if not most, of the great comedies of world literature are intimately close to tears—think of *The Misanthrope,* Kleist's *Amphitryon, The Cherry Orchard,* Shaw's *Pygmalion,* Giraudoux's *Intermezzo, The Good Woman of Setzuan, Waiting for Godot,* and almost any Shakespearean comedy, among others. There is considerable truth in Pauline Kael's summary of *Smiles of a Summer Night:* "In this vanished setting, nothing lasts, there are no winners in the game of love; all victories are ultimately defeats—only the game goes on." To be sure, Anne and Henrik seem to be privileged beings, emerging from the tussle and hypocrisies as joyful winners. In Bergman's loveliest stage direction, we read about their reaction to the hostile merriment at the dinner party: "Everyone laughs but Henrik and Anne. They are quiet and embarrassed in the presence of this gaiety without happiness." And a little later, after Henrik has tried, ineptly and boorishly but sincerely, to shake up these two-faced banterers, the camera shows him from the back, humbly apologizing to them. Henrik's black suit, as he stands there with arms outstretched in front of that glittering assembly, makes him look like a large ebony crucifix exhorting these shallow pleasure-seekers with a vision of suffering. Yet for all this virtue, love, and purifying pain of Henrik's and Anne's, for all their being among those rare young lovers scarce enough to be counted on the fingers of one's hands, can we be sure that Fredrik and Desirée, or even Malcolm and Charlotte and old Mrs. Armfeldt, were not, once upon a time, just like these unblemished creatures?

There is no clear answer to this question in the film, except, perhaps, an ironic implication in those three smiles of *the* summer night (Robin Wood rightly insists that the article in the film's title should be the definite one, meaning *the* summer night, universal and absolute). The first smile, to recapitulate, is for young lovers; the second, "for the clowns, the fools, the incorrigible"; the third, "for the grieving, the sleepless, the ones who have lost their way, the frightened, the lonely." The question, the final and unanswered question of the film, is whether the three general conditions to which the three smiles address themselves are to be taken as simultaneous but separate, or, as the stages of the dawn follow one another, as successive phases like the seven ages of man. Are some people happy lovers, others insouciant buffoons, and still others sad, abandoned, and lost? Or are these merely three consecutive stages of the brief summer's night and day that are human life?

One view would be absolutist, the other relativist. And the relativist outlook is strongly suggested by a charming little scene—another one where somebody watches other people, in the present case through a door. Fredrik, from the dark hall, is observing Henrik reading and preaching to Petra in his lighted room. *"Henrik: Why does temptation have a beautiful face, and why is the straight and narrow path so rocky? Can you tell me why? Petra: I guess it's because you need something nice to look at when you knock yourself out there among the stones."* Henrik, disgusted, shakes his head; but, behind him in the darkness, his father shakes *his* head —shakes it at his son's head-shake. Superficially, Henrik has hold of the gospel truth. But, beneath it, there is Petra's shrewd common sense; behind it, Fredrik's worldly wisdom. So Miss Kael seems justified in concluding her piece on *Smiles* by quoting the Swedish critic Rune Waldekranz, who writes that the film "wears the costume of the fin de siècle period for visual emphasis of the erotic comedy's fundamental premise—that the step between the sublime and the ridiculous in love is a short one, but nevertheless one that a lot of people stub their toes on. Although benefiting from several ingenious slapstick situations, *Smiles of a Summer Night* is a comedy in the most important meaning of the word. It is an arabesque on an essentially tragic theme, that of man's insufficiency, at the same time as it wittily illustrates the belief expressed fifty years ago by Hjalmar Söderberg that the only absolutes in life are 'the desire of the flesh and the incurable loneliness of the soul.' " *

In a highly theatrical film of this kind (Renoir's *The Rules of the Game* and Carné and Prévert's *The Children of Paradise* are other brilliant examples), ensemble acting is of the utmost importance. It redounds to Bergman's glory that he has goaded his already superb repertory-company actors into surpassing themselves— whether through the coruscation of his writing or of his direction, or both. Gunnar Björnstrand's Egerman—with his Renaissance beard, his slender, droopy mustache, and short hair with something like bangs in front—is a dapper, sardonic, clever, risible, touching figure. The chameleon contradictions of his personality are perhaps best caught in Desirée's apostrophe: "You old goat, you brute, you long-nosed camel, how unusually human you look." Björnstrand's many-faceted, mercurial, thoroughly complacent yet also vulnerable characterization allows us to laugh with and at him, to weep for him and for all of errant humanity through him—

* *I Lost It at the Movies* (Boston: Atlantic Monthly Press, 1965). Miss Kael might have added that the Söderberg dictum comes from his play *Gertrud* (1906), which was made into a film by Carl Dreyer, one of Bergman's spiritual ancestors.

not just successively but virtually at once. When he takes his little nap with Anne before the theatre and dreams about Desirée, the screenplay calls for him to look, while asleep, "like a dead king on a sarcophagus—a dead king who is satisfied with his death." Gunnar Björnstrand, great artist that he is, carries off that tall order, so to speak, in his sleep.

He is matched all the way by Eva Dahlbeck's Desirée, mature yet coyly girlish, sophisticated yet forthright, actressy yet genuine, Junoesque yet graceful, formidable but also lovably affectionate. Although she handles herself like a clever actress both on and off stage, what she affects and what she is are, very humanly, allowed to diverge visibly from time to time. How splendidly Miss Dahlbeck enacts the small but piercing epiphanies Bergman has dropped into the screenplay no more conspicuously than a hintingly quizzical inflection in an even-keeled conversation. When, for example, she is taking her curtain calls after the play (we watch with Fredrik from the wings—yet another of those unmasking vantage points, like windows or open doors): what a difference between the harried, fidgety woman, nervously fussing and preening behind the lowered curtain, and the radiant, gracious goddess, serenely beaming and curtseying at her ecstatic audience the moment the curtain is up! And, again, how enchantingly addlepated this self-possessed woman can be when Egerman tries to interrupt her sarcastic broadside at him—"No!" she cries, "I'll do the talking and when I talk, I'll talk even if I have nothing to say, but I am so furious with you that I forgot what I was thinking about and that's so typical of you. Well, what were you going to say?" Eva Dahlbeck conveys this imperious illogic with such vulnerability protruding under its overbearing absurdity as to make her—here as elsewhere in the film—the embodiment of feminine irresistibility. Is it the folly of the emotions or the wisdom of the flesh that can so drolly defy mere reasonableness?

Scarcely less splendid are the others: Ulla Jacobsson, fragile and childlike, exuding inner and outer loveliness, and finding at crucial moments, as if by accident, the tones of innate womanly strength; Jarl Kulle, as Malcolm, arrogant militarist and Don Juan (the two practically identical Janus faces), but with a brazenness that is not quite unappealing and a seductiveness that cannot disguise an underlying awareness of the hollowness of the masquerade—as in that hopeful-hopeless laugh with which he promises his wife to be faithful until the "great yawn" separates them.* What Kulle is especially good at conveying is a kind of pompousness so theatrical as to make us suspect a put-on; whereas at other times he can look quite genuinely the victim of his boundless preoccupation with himself.

How perfect, too, is Margit Carlquist as his exacerbated wife. The actress manages to keep us constantly guessing whether she is more sinning or sinned against, whether she is a born wildcat or merely a desperate wife clawing her way toward what is decently due her. And how moving she is in the gossiping scene with Anne, when, just after she has bitchily betrayed Fredrik's ostensible infidelity, she suddenly throws off all disguises and becomes herself: loving, crying, hating, wretched—and not caring who knows and deplores it. Miss Carlquist, looking a little too predatory to be beautiful, but burning with a glacial fire, becomes, of a sudden, utterly defenseless and heartbreaking. It is, for me, one of the finest moments in the history of film.

Superb, too, is Harriet Andersson's Petra, a minx with a heart, not of gold but of flesh and blood, which is better. Temperamental, cajoling, saucy, and innocent by turns, Miss Andersson succeeds in conveying the same complexities as the upper-class females, but, as it were, toned down to a homelier, earthier scale, yet entrancing for it. The ingenuous pleasure with which, upon being scolded for it by Henrik, she notes in the mirror the hip-swinging lasciviousness of her walk easily draws us into her own delight. Opposite her, Åke Fridell is a Frid full of swagger and impudence, marvelously nonchalant as he finishes his beer before getting around to ready the carriage for Anne's and Henrik's escape, and still, like all the other men in the film, putty in the hands of the canny women who are domineering and cruel only to be kind. Admittedly, Björn Bjelvenstam is somewhat unduly clumsy as Henrik, not quite able to project the romantic underneath the bumbler, but his is easily the most thankless role.

A final accolade is owed to those three elderly graces, out of and above it all: Naima Wifstrand as a sublimely egotistic yet shrewdly perceptive Mrs. Armfeldt ("Sometimes I admire your muddled astuteness," her daughter compliments her); Jullan Kindahl as the faithful old cook of the Egermans, brimful of quiet

---

* The far from satisfactory printed English translation by Lars Malmstrom and David Kushner at this point particularly misleadingly reads "the last gasp." This loses the *double-entendre:* faithful unto death, or, more likely, insuperable boredom.

authority, saturninely critical both of Petra's attempts at upward mobility and of Anne's officious and bootless slumming in the kitchen; and Gull Natorp's Malla, Desirée's well-meaning but sharp-tongued dresser, a walking show-business cliché, but redeemed by intelligent underplaying.

Smiles of a Summer Night occupies a central position in Bergman's *oeuvre*. If that were the purpose of this study, I could easily show how it recapitulates many of his earlier themes and foreshadows a number of his later concerns. But for my present purpose it should suffice to reiterate more emphatically what I have already stated: in a relatively short compass and with a very modest cast of characters, Bergman here explores virtually the entire range of human love, from youthful adoration to avuncularly sentimental benevolence; from neurotic, vengeful passion to easeful indulgence of the appetites; from foot-stamping, infantile capriciousness to wistful, autumnal resignation. And the wonder of it is that these and other aspects of love and carnality are not narrowly and rigorously confined to the characters in whom they predominate, but are allowed to crop up in antipodal psyches. The film is instinct with playful sagacity and bittersweet grace, and is truly ecumenical in its concerns. It is, finally, a paean to what Petra, with unwitting, instinctual perspicacity, labels as "something nice to look at when you knock yourself out there among the stones." And that may well be the most pointedly succinct periphrasis for love.

WINTER LIGHT

Winter Light is in many ways Bergman's most extraordinary film. I shall not try to fill in here the gap between *Smiles of a Summer Night* and *Winter Light,* which came out in 1963. Into this period fall the films that made Bergman's tremendous international reputation, most particularly *The Seventh Seal* and *Wild Strawberries,* films that I can admire but not love, which, along with *The Magician* (really *The Face*), have contributed much to giving Bergman, besides his fame, a certain bad repute. For, with greater or lesser right, these films could be accused of stuffiness, pretentiousness, or metaphysical maundering. But with *Through a Glass Darkly* (1961), Bergman set out on a new path, that of the "chamber film," a term derived both from Strindberg's "chamber plays" and from their common ancestor, chamber music. In this kind of filmmaking (and the so-called trilogy—*Through a Glass Darkly, Winter Light,* and *The Silence*—is the first example of it in Bergman's work, though later films fit into the same mould), the cast of characters usually does not exceed four or five, the action is confined in time and space, and the story is intensely intimate, although larger implications are by no means excluded—if anything, they are invited.

In *Through a Glass Darkly,* Bergman had concluded with a rather facile equation between love and God as a solution to human problems; yet the heroine's madness seemed precisely based on some guilt connected with religion and the concept of a terrible, even obscene, God who assumes the loathed shape of a spider. The cozy God-is-love ending was an oversimplification that Bergman came to regret bitterly and promptly set about correcting. (He was, accordingly, very much against inclusion of that film in this book, and urged the choice of *Winter Light* in its stead.) The antidote emerged sixteen months later as *The Communicants* or, as retitled in England and America, *Winter Light.* This is the one case where I shall keep the English title, though divergent from the original, for my discussion; first, because it seems to me as good as the Swedish one, and, secondly, because the word "communicants" falls so unpleasingly on our ears.

Winter Light is one of the shortest (eighty minutes), starkest, and most uncompromising of Bergman's films. One has the feeling here that no concession whatever was made to the audience's desires and presumed needs: a truth Bergman wanted to convey is presented in àll its darkness, quasi-sterility, and lack of comic or aesthetic relief. Even the plot is minimal—probably the most stripped of story elements in Bergman's *oeuvre.* For this reason alone, *Winter Light* tends to be, on first viewing, a disconcerting film. But it is not a case of using bleakness and denudedness merely as a form of novelty with which to jolt us, or of disappointing us through failure to reach an intended goal. *Winter Light* cleaves relentlessly to its purpose and vision, and does not even stop to consider whether anyone or anything beyond the artist and his materials is involved in the equation that is art.

The film takes place between noon and 3:00 P.M. on a late November Sunday. The time is significant: winter has only just begun, and there is more and worse to come. The film is in three movements: (1) the morning service at Mittsunda's medieval church, and the events immediately following and taking place in the sacristy or in the church itself; (2) at the site of the fisherman's suicide by the roaring rapids, at the schoolhouse, at the house of the fisherman's widow, on the way to Frostnäs; (3) at the more modern (nineteenth-century) Frostnäs church, the events leading up to the service, the beginning of Vespers. Bergman himself has described these three movements as (1) the smashing of the coda of *Through a Glass Darkly,* settling with the secure, wish-fulfillment God, (2) emptiness after the smashing, (3) the awakening of a new faith.* It is interesting to note, too, that the duration of the

* Quoted after Birgitta Steene, *Ingmar Bergman* (New York: Twayne Publishers, 1968). Miss Steene, in turn, is quoting from Vilgot Sjöman's *L 136. Dagbok med Ingmar Bergman,* Sjöman's diary while he was working as an assistant to Bergman on *Winter Light.*

All photographs in this chapter courtesy Janus Films.

The Communion service:
Pastor Tomas Ericsson: "Send
down thy Holy Spirit to our
hearts, that he may kindle a
living faith within us and
prepare us rightly to celebrate
the memory of our Savior
. . . who in the same night
that he was betrayed, took
bread; and when he had given
thanks, he brake it, and gave
it to his disciples, saying:
'Take, eat. This is my Body
which is given for you: Do this
in remembrance of me.' "

*"The Body of our Lord Jesus Christ, which was
given for thee."*

film approximates the time covered by the film. *Winter Light* strives
to be as naturalistic as decently possible.

The beginning, like the end, of the film takes place during a
church service. The screen play calls for "a gray half-light," and
a grayish quality seems to emanate from the entire film, even from
the outdoor scenes in which the snow-covered ground seems to
reflect the sky's grayness. Here in the church at noon the Reverend
Tomas Ericsson is approaching the end of the morning service. At
first he seems merely dour, but the recurrent close-ups reveal a
discomfort, an arduously overmastered pain in his eyes: the man
is ill, or emotionally disturbed. The church itself is stark, with a
sixteenth-century Flemish carved altarpiece, a triptych whose central panel represents the Trinity, with a relatively small crucified
Christ cradled between the immense knees of the Father. The
congregation consists of nine people, all of whom are representa-
tive specimens.

Two men are there more or less ex officio: Knut Aronsson, the
church warden here at Mittsunda; and the hunchback Algot Frövik,
sexton at Frostnäs, where Reverend Ericsson will preach Vespers.
There is also the couple, Jonas and Karin Persson, seemingly quite
ordinary people. (A marvelous make-up job turns the handsome
and aristocratic Max von Sydow into a plain, peasanty figure, and
the sophisticatedly sexy Gunnel Lindblom into a simple and almost
homely woman.) They seem out of place, somewhat ill at ease in
church. Then there is an old man who carefully follows the text in
his prayer book, and an elderly woman who seems positively
thrilled to be there. But a middle-aged mother's participation is

146

rather a matter of routine, and her brat of a small daughter is un-
interested in the whole thing: dozes off, plays with her Teddy bear,
or licks the wood of the pews. Finally, there is the schoolteacher,
Märta Lundberg, frumpish and seemingly unfeminine (the lovely
Ingrid Thulin brilliantly made-down and acting the part of the plain
woman, including an ungainly, mannish walk that can be deeply
moving in context); her attitude here is subtly ironic and provocative. This psychic diversity becomes manifest during the Communion scene that follows, where Bergman shows each communicant
in successive close-up—avid, awkward, unconvinced, or skeptical
—and suggests with utmost economy the various attitudes and
personalities. All this takes some fifteen minutes, during which
there is no dialogue except for a tiny "Thanks!" from the pregnant
Mrs. Persson to Märta, who helps her back on her feet after Communion. Otherwise the sound track is taken up with hymn-singing,
organ music, and the words of the service. The very first of these
words we hear are: "Lift up your hearts to God." The irony of this
strikes us only in retrospect: it is spoken by the depressed Tomas,
who feels abandoned by God, and, since the death of his wife, cannot lift up his heart in love toward anyone. And it is spoken to a
congregation that, by and large, is in no mood or condition for
heart-lifting: even the organist reads magazines between bored
bouts with his instrument.

The Communion sequence is brilliantly staged and photographed. Since Robin Wood has described it perfectly, let me
quote him at length: "The receiving of the bread and the receiving
of the wine are shot in quite different ways. During the former,

147

"Christ's blood, shed for thee."

filmed in a single take, the camera is behind the communicants; we watch Tomas pass from one to the other with the plate of wafers, each time uttering the words about Christ's body, with an increasing awareness of their meaninglessness to him, so that it is as if the formula must be deliberately forced out. The concentration demanded by the continuous take makes us *feel* every hesitation. The receiving of the wine is shown in a series of close-ups in which each communicant is subtly characterized in relation to the Communion: the sexton closes his eyes after drinking; the old countrywoman is the only one of the five who places her hands over the priest's on the chalice, not self-conscious about physical contact, wholly intent on the sacrament; Jonas Persson keeps his eyes lowered throughout—the chalice has to be put exactly to his lips, and he drinks in a clumsy and passive way; his wife looks up at the priest with an ingratiating and apologetic smile, as if pleading for reassurance. The essential of each character is thus economically suggested: only Märta—the only one filmed in profile —is enigmatic here."

This is accurate observation as well as astute evaluation. But Wood may be reading a little more into the scene than is readily apparent: I doubt whether Tomas's increasing awareness of the meaninglessness of the ritual is conveyed by anything specific— though, as I said, a general malaise can be detected in his expression and, perhaps, tone. What Bergman has done here is comparable to the Dadaists' procedure with the *objet trouvé:* you take a church service and Communion and transpose them, more or less untampered with, onto the screen; in the changed context, they affect the viewer in a new and different way. Here, on film,

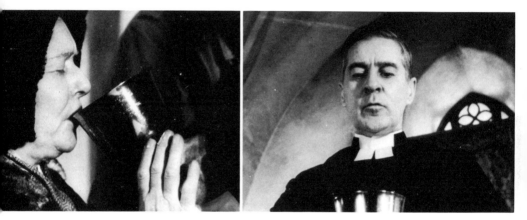

"Christ's blood, shed for thee."

where the audience is eager for the story to get under way, the long lingering over something seemingly formulaic and predictable becomes irritating, even painful. But, at the same time, it primes the viewer for closer watchfulness and detection of whatever detail departs from the norm, goes beyond the mere documentary aspect of the scene. In this way the tone is set, and we are prepared for a film whose action will take place in minute particulars, nuances, overtones, facial tremors that are symptomatic of upheavals in the depths of the soul.

A device that Bergman uses to good effect throughout is the implicit comment that some physical disability makes on a situation or dialogue that it punctuates. So at the very moment Tomas mentions "eternal life," the screenplay notes that "a wave of fever passes through the clergyman's head and he draws a deep breath." Similarly, coughing fits coming at crucial points provide an ironic commentary. Wood points to the organist's strategic

"Christ's blood, shed for thee."

yawns during the service, and to Aronsson's, the warden's, coughing "in the middle of the singing, more from boredom than illness." Even mere glances can be very significant here, and convey more than Wood notices in his otherwise sharp analysis. Thus when Tomas offers Märta the wafer, she smiles at him ironically, but he refuses to meet her gaze. Later, by way of an exquisite little revenge, Märta averts her face (hence the profile shot Wood mentions) and keeps Tomas waiting when he comes to her with the chalice. I am reminded here of what Bergman once said about film-making: "I can't help thinking that I am working with an instrument so refined that, with it, it would be possible for us to illuminate the human soul with an infinitely more vivid light, to unmask it even more brutally and to annex to our field of knowledge new domains of reality." * This aim is relentlessly pursued in the film's following scenes.

* From an article by Bergman originally published in *Cahiers du Cinéma* (July 1956), and translated and reprinted in *Film Makers on Film Making*, Harry M. Geduld, ed. (Bloomington: Indiana University Press, 1967).

The service is over and the sick and suffering Tomas retires to the vestry, to the accompaniment of the voluntary, which the organist, Blom, plays at the hastiest tempo. Aronsson follows the minister with the collection in a bag at the end of a pole, and the careful emptying of this bag, the counting of its paltry contents, the transferral of them into another bag, which is ceremonially tied up, and the meticulous recording of the sum in a ledger constitute another, secular ritual that comments wryly on the one just over. Tomas tries to make himself comfortable in a worn armchair, extracts from his briefcase some biscuits and a Thermos flask, out of which he pours coffee into a cracked cup. The biscuits and the coffee are a secular echo of the bread and wine. Meanwhile Aronsson suggests that Tomas get a substitute minister for the afternoon service at Frostnäs and a much-needed permanent housekeeper—Märta, the schoolteacher, who, as it later develops, is Tomas's mistress. The pastor rejects both suggestions: his obstinate refusal of any form of solicitude is clearly related to his in-

"Christ's blood, shed for thee."

ability to tender any. This is an aspect of one of the main themes of the trilogy, as well as of Bergman's later films: the problem of mutual help. What succor can we give one another out of love, or friendship, or just common humanity?

In the scenes that take place in the vestry the lighting is of supreme importance. There is only one rather narrow window occupying the entire height and width of a sort of alcove that starts at elbow level. The window has relatively small panes and is crisscrossed by staves; there are also bars just this side of the window, making for further crisscrossing. The walls of the vestry are roughly plastered, and the light in the alcove emphasizes their rugosities. The effect is that of a prison cell. A good many of the most intimate and searching shots have the camera peering in from just inside the window, suggesting the closeness, the confinement, within; other shots catch the characters from inside the room leaning into the alcove and toward the window: prisoners yearning for freedom. The light in the church is generally muted; in the vestry, it is aggressive and makes for strident contrasts. Bergman achieves marvelous effects by having a person in the vestry turn toward the light or away from it: faces light up with a hard glare, or are haloed from behind, or go into partial or total eclipse.

Algot Frövik comes into the vestry. He is a hunchback, a cripple; his head hangs forward, forcing his eyes to look up at you as if in supplication or, sometimes, mockery. Generally humble, this retired railroad worker turned sexton and verger at Frostnäs can, at times, exude a proud irony. He has a problem to discuss, but Reverend Ericsson tells him impatiently that he will talk to him after the service at Frostnäs. Frövik is followed by a much bigger

"Christ's blood, shed for thee."

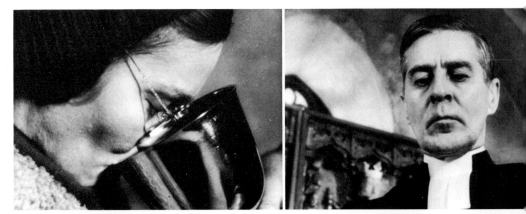

challenge to the physically and psychically tormented Tomas: the Perssons, with Jonas's problem.

The beginning of the ensuing three-way conversation is, as Robin Wood correctly observed, grotesque, almost comical. While Mrs. Persson tries to explain her husband's perplexedness, Jonas doesn't speak; he merely looks down, locked in a stubborn, unhappy silence. His face tends to be more in the light than his wife's, as if there were something burning, feverish about it; hers is usually nearer the camera, as if her solicitude and bewilderment were meant to concern us more immediately. Finally she manages to convey that Jonas has read somewhere about the Chinese soon having their own atom bomb, and how, seeing that they are economically desperate and trained to hate and fight, they will surely use it. And there is something infinitely touching about the postscript Karin Persson attaches to her faltering narrative after a pause: "I don't worry too much. That must be because I haven't much imagination. But Jonas thinks about it all the time. We turn the matter over this way and that. Though, of course, I can't be of much help. We've three children—besides the one that's on its way, of course." How moving it is for this woman to claim lack of imagination as the reason for not sharing her husband's excessive, morbid fear! And there is something like pride in the way she describes her husband's "superior" fixation. Then there are those embarrassed little "of course"s with which she tries to normalize her narrative, reduce the eerie to the conversational. Lastly, there is her appeal to motherhood and pregnancy as an excuse for what she considers to be her uselessness to her husband—a weak excuse as she sees it, but a very good one as we do. This is the Bergmanian woman: steadier, stronger, earthier than her man.

A masterly scene follows. As a visual refrain, a crucifix is glimpsed from time to time on the wall opposite the window. "It is a crude, roughly carved image of the suffering Christ," the screenplay comments, "ineptly made. The mouth opens in a scream, the arms are grotesquely twisted, the hands convulsively clutch the nails, the brow is bloody beneath the thorns, and the body arches outward, as if trying to tear itself away from the wood. The image smells of fungus, mouldy timber. Its paint is flaking off in long strips." The description is overwrought, including even smell; but such is the power of Bergman's direction, abetted by Nykvist's cinematography, that all of this comes across on the

Let us praise the Lord.

154

screen. Between the sparse, chilling light seeping in through the window and the anguished crucifix (how different from the one in the church, where God the Father protectively holds up the cross to which his son is nailed), Tomas Ericsson looks more and more desperate in his attempts to help Jonas with such platitudes as "We all go about with the same dread—more or less" and "We must trust in God." At first, the fisherman's reaction is increased panic. But gradually he comes to look straight ahead of him rather than shamefacedly at the floor; he is staring the world down with the luminous, mad truth by which he is possessed. As Tomas gets more and more rattled in his efforts to argue a message of hope in which he himself no longer believes, Jonas quietly becomes more exultant in his insane certainty. He smiles pityingly at Tomas, who insists that despite God's remoteness and our helplessness and fear, "we must go on living." Jonas looks at him with that gaze of the mad Vincent van Gogh, as Jacques Prévert evoked it: *"Il a le regard bleu et doux / Le vrai regard lucide et fou."* "Why must we go on living?" he asks.

"Because we must. We have a responsibility," says Tomas, who cannot find words of love, only of duty. Jonas replies: "You are not well, Vicar," and the roles are forthwith exchanged: the man in mortal dread is concerned for the parson. When Tomas proposes that they just sit there and say whatever comes into their heads, Jonas replies that it can't be: he and Karin must get back to look after the children. Is this a last flaring up of some paternal, human feeling, or only an excuse to get away and closer to sui-

Bergman interrupts the flow of the surface happenings with the symbols of what lies beneath. (See Persona, *pages 242 and 243.)*

e your hearts to God
receive the blessing.

The Lord bless you and keep you

the Lord let his face shine upon you

"The Lord bless you and keep you.
The Lord let his face shine upon you . . .
and give you peace."

cide? Finally, the vicar and the wife extract a promise from Jonas that he will come back after driving Karin home, and the couple depart in a hurry. Tomas goes into the church. Outside, the weather is worsening: wind, snow, cold. The minister stands by the altar and looks up at the huge image of God with Christ between his knees and the dove fluttering on top. He finds it, as he exclaims, absurd.

At the far end of the church, Märta has come in. Her first words are that she brought Tomas something hot. His answer is again a polite rejection: he walks back into the vestry telling her that he himself has brought coffee from home, even though that coffee has long since turned cold. Tomas's inability to receive is reiterated, but Märta's lack of grace is also underscored: no sooner has she deposited her basket and unbuttoned her mannish sheepskin coat than she has to fumble for a handkerchief and loudly blow her nose.

There follows an image superbly contrasting with the preceding one in which Tomas stood alone in the large darkling church. Now he "goes up to the little prison window of the vestry, leans his elbow on its broad stone sill. She stands beside him, puts her arm around his shoulder and draws him to herself." The light beats strongly in their faces. But this light is even less consoling than the darkness. It hardens Tomas's features, emphasizes Märta's charmlessness. And the ensuing colloquy is miserably curt and dry: "*Märta:* What is it, Tomas? *Tomas:* To you, nothing. *Märta:* Tell me, even so. *Tomas:* God's silence. *Märta (wonderingly):* God's

and give you peace.

silence? *Tomas:* Yes. (*Long pause*) God's silence." And there follows a yet longer pause during which they look at the falling snow. There is something awful about that staccato of stichomythic exchange that ends with the thrice repeated "God's silence," capped by a long human silence. The thickening snow in front, the prison cell behind, and, in the middle, these two unsuccessful lovers in the cold winter light. God has failed Tomas, and he, in turn, has failed Märta. Again he rejects her solicitude when she finds his brow feverish and suggests he take to his bed. Instead, he questions her about why she came to Communion. "It's supposed to be a love-feast, isn't it?" Märta replies, and asks whether he has read her letter yet. No, he hasn't had the time. There is no love in Communion—not for Tomas, anyway; and there is no communion in love, at least not for these lovers.

Tomas has her letter with him, though; but it is thick and he figures it to be something unpleasant. Furthermore, why write, when they see each other daily? "We go astray when we talk," Märta answers. So there is a built-in noncommunication, a silence, in their very speech. Once again, poor Märta tries to make Tomas marry her; once again, he becomes evasive. She hastily interprets his evasion: he doesn't love her, besides which she doesn't believe in God one bit. She persists, however, and tries to disguise her dreadful anxiety with self-depreciation. Even so, it all tumbles out with naked, pitiful urgency. Here Blom, the organist, interrupts, looking for some sheet music; his intrusion is an embarrassment, and, after his departure, the mood is exacerbated. Märta is

*The closing hymn: we hear the inspirational words
and see the reality. Organist Blom looks at his watch.*

finally driven to mock Tomas's worries: "God doesn't speak. God hasn't ever spoken, because he doesn't exist. It's all so unusually, so horribly simple." At the same time, she kisses him, and tells him he must learn to love. But he dismisses this with a bit of sarcasm, inquiring whether she'll be the one to teach him. With a wry smile, she declares: "It's beyond me. I haven't the strength." And she leaves.

The scene is a fine portrayal of the minor-key quarrels of a dying relationship, and a preparation for the great showdown to come later, at the schoolhouse. Here the gloves are still on, the rules of civilized sparring are still observed. Such scenes of attrition between lovers are Bergman's specialty, and he handles them superlatively. What is most extraordinary, though, is that, however many of them there are in his films, or even in a single film, none unduly resembles the others, and each commands our renewed concern and respect. Antonioni, too, is an expert at such scenes, but in Bergman they cut deeper; one can see Corrado and Giulia in *L'Avventura* accommodate themselves through infidelities to their marriage of mutual resentment; in the later Bergman films, the wounds bleed too much for such relatively simple solutions.

Next, Tomas is alone with the surrounding objects: the grisly crucifix; the dour, old-fashioned clock that ticks away with, as Bergman says, a life of its own; a coat of arms, featuring a skull and crossbones, inside the church; the falling snow to be glimpsed outside; the hard, resounding stroke of one from the clock. Jonas must come, the minister tells himself in great anxiety. At length,

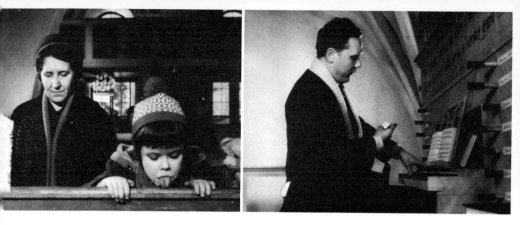

he sits down in the vestry again, takes out of his wallet Märta's letter, and cannot help taking out some pictures of his dead wife as well. Here a Bergmanian master touch: the pictures have RAKOPIA (rough print, photographer's proof) stamped across the woman's forehead. There is something exceptionally gripping about this: that the only pictures of his adored wife Tomas seems to possess should be so disfiguringly marked. There is a strong suggestion of transience about this, and of our unawareness of our transience: we don't bother to have proper pictures taken of the one we love, and suddenly it's too late—we're left with an imperfect image, rather like a faulty, faded memory.

Tomas sighs, "My darling," and puts the pictures away; unwillingly, he begins to read Märta's letter. With this sequence, Bergman took one of his biggest risks: almost the entire letter is spoken by Märta in close-up, with the camera immobilized while all of Märta's anguish, complaints, faint hopes come tumbling out. This continuous take lasts some five minutes, with only Ingrid Thulin's sensitive and deeply sincere facial play, her expressive line readings, and the slight movements of her head to hold our attention and provide variety. We begin with Tomas reading; later, there is one cut away to Tomas and Märta decorating the altar with flowers at a time when her severe eczema came between them. Otherwise, it is all Märta speaking, pleading, remonstrating, yearning. It is all a subdued hysterical outburst, a lament muted by diffidence. Jörn Donner considers the flashback a mistake; I don't. It brings us back to the same spot where Tomas dourly offered

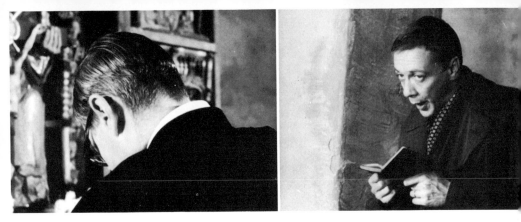

The pastor moves from one ritual to another.
Aronsson counts the collection.
Algot Frövik seeks to communicate with the pastor
(see picture 4, page 154), but the pastor brushes him
off until later. He has refused the opportunity.

Holy Communion to Märta, who accepted it with a certain irony. Now it is human communion that is shown breaking down. The sameness of locale suggests a possible relationship between the two failures of communication—perhaps, indeed, their ultimate identity.

The flashback, in fact, is a powerfully suggestive scene that had to be visualized, dramatized. We must see Märta's bandaged hands, as if she were wearing mittens to protect her against Tomas's coldness—and, surely, the eczema may be psychosomatic. Perhaps a better analogy would be to frostbite, frostbite incurred by touching Tomas's icy heart. Märta asks Tomas defiantly to pray for her and for her hands, something that never occurred to him, even though he says he believes in the efficacy of prayer. But when Märta tears off her bandages, Tomas is nauseated and cannot pray. We are back now to Märta narrating: we hear of the eczema breaking out virulently on her forehead and, later, on her hands again and on her feet. Further on in her letter, Märta remarks: "One thing in particular I couldn't understand: your peculiar indifference to Jesus Christ." The Swedish critics cited by Birgitta Steene who saw parallels between Märta (Martha) and the biblical servant woman, and between Märta and Christ because of her selfless love, quasi-stigmata and age (thirty-three—Christ's at the time of his passion), seem to me on the right track. But Tomas rejects this redemption through woman's love just as he

Just a cold.

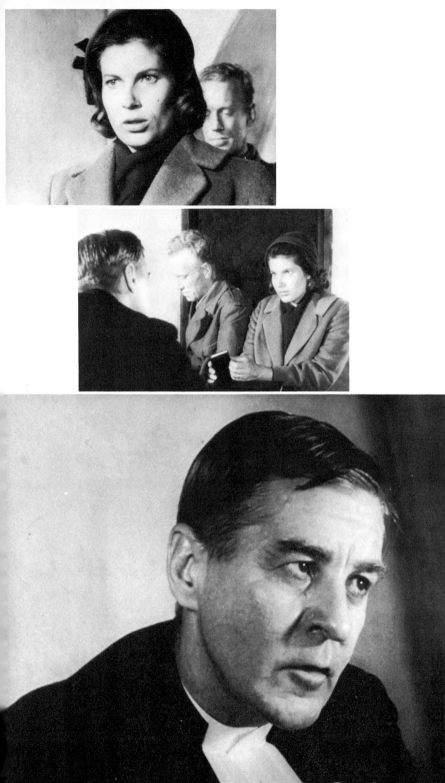

We must trust God.

*Faced with the reality of
Jonas Persson's anguish,
Tomas delivers pious
banalities.
Jonas's face is bathed in
the strong light from outside. (Bergman has referred
to the light as being the
protagonist.)*

always rejected Christ in his religion. And at this time of the stigmata the two years' relationship between Tomas and Märta ceased to be physical.

Märta, like her family, has never taken Christianity seriously. God and Christ existed only "as vague notions" and Märta is convinced that "life is problematic enough as it is . . . without supernatural elements." (This remark closely resembles Bergman's words in the interview with me: "Things are difficult enough without God.") Nevertheless, Märta prayed—since Tomas wouldn't—for herself. And she asked God: "If there is a purpose in my suffering, tell me what it is. And I'll bear my pain without complaining. I'm strong." Much later, her eczema gone, Märta understood that the cause of her pain was Tomas; that the terrible task she had to grapple with was his lovelessness. And she burned with gratitude to whatever the cause of her love might have been, God or her biological functions. From this we may conclude that God and Christ are only metaphors—but useful ones—for insight, understanding, dedication of oneself to another. God may not, as the father in *Through a Glass Darkly* simplistically tells his son, be love; but love may be God, may be an analogue for the divine, the only available form of transcendence.

Bergman must have derived this monologue from the interview scene in Truffaut's *The 400 Blows*. But Truffaut used jump cuts to suggest the passage of time, showed the boy Antoine in medium close-up less relentless than a tight shot, and mitigated the rigor of the soliloquy by allowing us to hear the questions of the woman psychologist. Bergman turned the device into something more uncompromising: the long take, the single person on screen, stationary camera, close-up. And it worked brilliantly, permitting him to play daring variations on it in the later films: *Persona, Hour of*

The Perssons leave Tomas in the confinement of the vestry.

the Wolf, Shame, and *A Passion* (*The Passion of Anna*).

Tomas falls into a feverish half-sleep now, overcome by anguish and exhaustion as well as influenza. "The tick of the vestry clock assumes the rhythm of a penitential lash," writes Peter Cowie somewhat flamboyantly but not wholly without justification. Suddenly, as if he were an apparition in a dream, Jonas Persson stands inside the vestry. As Tomas rouses himself from his dozing, Persson's face, lit from behind by the window, seems to be limned in light. In the conversation that follows, Tomas is usually seen with the agonizing Christ in back of him, whereas Jonas tends to be haloed from behind, as if he were a kind of Paraclete. It is like a confrontation of two Christs, or two aspects of Christ. And again, there is the Bergmanian irony: the would-be comforter fails, but the resultant death is part of his own awakening, if not, indeed, salvation.

At first, characteristically, Tomas makes awkward attempts to draw Jonas into an either innocuous or meaningful conversation, and fails at both. He finally hits on the idea of confessing to Jonas, reversing their presumptive roles. At first, Jonas is interested, but when Tomas tells him more and more about his overprotected childhood, his stay in Lisbon as a seamen's chaplain and ignoring the Civil War across the border to concentrate on his very own God, Jonas becomes uneasy: he doesn't want to hear about this. Yet it all comes tumbling out of Tomas: how he became a clergyman only to please his parents and give obedience where he couldn't give love. "So I became a clergyman and believed in God." Tomas thinks he is showing Jonas that the fisherman is not alone in his sense of isolation and fear, but his real need is to unburden himself. He confesses that the God he believed in was a private, fatherly one who loved all mankind but most of all him.

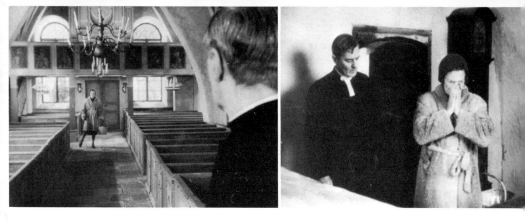

Bergman has been alternating
long shots between the
pastor's end of the church—
the altar—and the entrance,
between the communicants'
view and that of the pastor.
Here the pastor views Märta,
framed by the big windows
filled with light, as she viewed
him earlier during the service,
framed by the altar. Illumination comes from outside.
(See page 180.)
Märta confronts him with yet
another reality—his own life.
What ails him, she asks.
God's silence, he replies.
She has sent him a letter; has
he read it? No; again he has
not had time.

Poor Thomas.

At this point he is racked by a severe coughing fit, as it were underlining the preposterousness of his former notions: a God who was supposed to protect him against the fear of both death and life is letting him cough out his guts. As the confession proceeds, Jonas gets progressively more frightened.

For Jonas, it appears, there is no comfort in finding a fellow sufferer, a companion in abandonment. And Tomas continues: "Every time I confronted God with the reality I saw, he became ugly, revolting, a spider-God—a monster." The image of the spider-God, as has been duly noted, is of capital importance for Bergman, beginning with *Through a Glass Darkly:* a God not only loathsome as the spider is to man, but also deadly as he is to his victim trapped in his web and about to be sucked dry. And we see now, as Jonas recoils from all this, what Bergman's two men represent.

In the silent dark prison of the vestry, he waits out time— until Jonas comes.

Tomas is clearly a doubting Thomas, the least believing of Jesus' followers. He repeats, probably unconsciously, what Märta told him about himself: that in the midst of his late wife's mothering he was alone with his indifference to the gospel message, his jealous hatred of Jesus—exactly like Thomas the Doubter. Jonas seems to be none other than Jonah, the unhappy fellow swallowed by a whale—the engulfing, black fear of the atomic explosion, of the world that seems too much or too little for him. This fear is unmitigated by his wife, Karin, who is decent and not overprotective but also simple and unimaginative. Jonah, the supremely unlucky one, must in his hour of direst need stumble on this doubting, disbelieving, ravaged Tomas, an even greater failure as a man than as a priest. When Jonas tries to leave, Tomas becomes more frantic in his attempts at consolation.

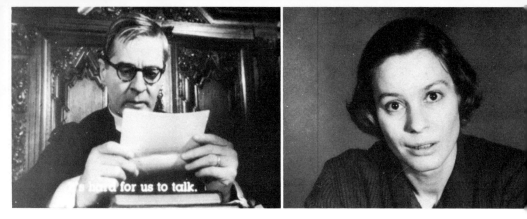

Märta's letter: the almost unbearably long take of Märta's face directly confronting the viewer forces the viewer into Tomas's position, to receive the reality of the woman on the screen. (See Persona, *page 221.)*

Tomas, in fact, closes the door to the church, as it were shutting Jonas into the vestry, the belly of the whale. And, ironically, Tomas stands under the crucifix as he intones his denial of God. Proudly he offers Jonas the best he has to give: his disbelief, his atheism. When one has realized that there is no creator to hold the world together, one can live undizzied by "immeasurable thought to make one's head spin." In disguising our aloneness—but our aloneness *together*—from one another, we have betrayed our existential truth and assumed the "stink of an antique godliness," a "humiliating sense of sin." And from here on Tomas speaks with a simple directness of the joys of our transient life, invoking, among other things, the strawberry beds (or patches) that, ever since *Summerplay,* have recurred in Bergman's work as a symbol of contentment, of the joy in summer and in being alive. After evoking the earthly paradise to the still-unconvinced Jonas, the vicar concludes with the words, "We've given gifts to each other, haven't we? You've given me your fear and I've given you a god I've killed." Now this seems to me a sound, indeed moving argument, but it is undercut by an even worse access of Tomas's sickness, during which Jonas flees.

What has happened in this key scene of the film? According to Arthur Gibson, a professor of theology at the University of Toronto and Director of the Intitute of Astrotheology, "The sociological concern and involvement, the humanistically vapid cosmopolitan-

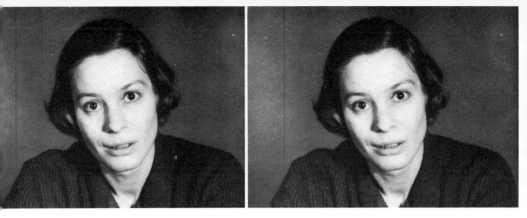

ism and Waldenism Tomas tries to evoke before Jonas—these are not enough." So Gibson contends in *The Silence of God,** a fanatically narrow-minded, singularly ill-written book, which sees all of Bergman's films as allegories of man's struggle toward God, and makes the entire Bergman *oeuvre* into a film-serial version of *Pilgrim's Progress.* Gibson refers sneeringly to "the faintly rotting strawberry beds of Pastor Tomas," though there is no such implication in Bergman. But we are to understand, I think, that Tomas is not yet fully convinced of the truth of his own words, and that Jonas, despairing, is merely confirmed in the validity of his death wish.

When Tomas comes to, no one is around. The screenplay reads: "God's silence, Christ's twisted face, the blood on the brow and hands, the soundless shriek behind the bared teeth." There is a paragraph break here, as in a prose poem, and a two-word line follows, short and awesome: "God's silence." Tomas moans: "God, my God, why have you forsaken me?" Almost unconsciously, he repeats Christ's words on the cross, identifying himself with the one in whom he has not really believed. Yet, paradoxically, this is also a blasphemous outcry, the beginning of his total rejection of God. He is in the church, leaning against the altar rail, and looking out at the ambiguous light beyond the tall church window. "I'm free now; free at last!" he exclaims, and is immediately shaken by

* New York: Harper & Row, 1969.

a terrible coughing fit that brings him to his knees. Märta, huddled against the dark wall by the window at which he gazed, has been observing him; now she rushes to him, kneels, and gathers him to her in a kind of *pietà.*

It would be possible to read this as a renewed humbling of Tomas by God, who forces him to his knees. But I think that the fact that Tomas looks out at the merciless winter light, that he collapses not out of genuflecting reverence before the immortal but out of mere mortal weakness, that he faces away from the altar when he sits down, and that the *pietà* takes the form of secular piety between him and his mistress, all suggest that the pastor is being reoriented toward humanity and human love as an end. But he has a long way to go as yet. When Märta offers to accompany him to Frostnäs for the evening service, he again rejects her kindness. At this point, the old woman we saw in church irrupts to announce that Jonas's body has just been found by the river: he shot himself through the head. It may be that this death contributes more than anything else to Tomas's awakening. In a sense, the halo that surrounded Jonas during his last talk with the minister was earned: besides being a Jonah, Jonas is also a bit of a Jesus.

The next episode, by the river, is the only one of any length to take us outdoors. But the snowy landscape is gray and cheerless, hemmed in further, as it were, by the roar of the rapids. The entire scene is in long-shot, excluding recognizable facial play; the noise of the waters almost completely obliterates the voices of Tomas and the police superintendent, excluding significant dialogue. Robin Wood evokes it accurately: "There is little sense of organized 'composition': a drab hopelessness, a sort of emotional paralysis, hangs over the whole sequence, and the seeming random-

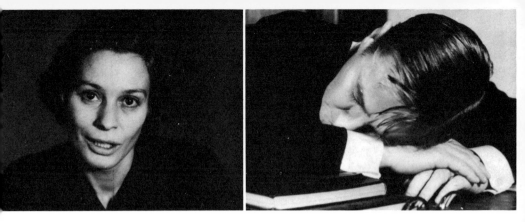

ness of everything emphasizes this. Throughout, a snowy drizzle falls, quite unbeautiful and undramatic, making the natural setting dull and undistinguished: not hostile to man's despair, but merely inanimate and material." Tomas performs the last rites over the slumped body mechanically: no overt emotion anywhere in the scene. This truly is winter light that flattens out everything: the living minister seems as distant, small, and bleak as the corpse itself. Is Tomas guilty of this man's death? Are they, in some sense, interchangeable? Have they somehow communicated—not in Holy Communion, not in conversation even, but as communicants in mortality: in Tomas's death-in-life and Jonas's real death? Is there a purpose in the near-rhyme, Jonas-Tomas?

It takes an Arthur Gibson to read this scene—and with it the meaning of the film itself—as perversely as this: "If a man is to be redeemed, it must be by the strong, desperate, rending *Caritas* of the God who cloaks himself in a dreadful silence in the face of all man's pertinent and impertinent questionings, who in this film speaks only once, in the majestic thunder of the waterfall that drowns out the solicitous chatter of the human establishment around the corpse of a suicide." There is, of course, no waterfall here, and no majestic thunder, only the persistent, dull noise of the rapids. And if God speaks here, it is only to Doctor Gibson.

Märta has walked down the road to join Tomas at the scene of death—he did not take her along in his car—but he makes her wait inside the vehicle. Now that the body has been removed, Tomas drives Märta back to the schoolhouse where she lives. Desperately in need of some aspirin, he follows Märta into the schoolhouse and, so as not to disturb the aunt who is visiting with her, waits in the classroom. While he sits on a school bench, a boy comes in with his dog to pick up a comic book he forgot inside his

*Tomas awakens to see that
Jonas has arrived.
The light from outside
brightens around Jonas.*

Not much fishing at this time of year.

Tomas: "Not much fishing at
this time of year.
"How long have you been
going about with this idea of
taking your own life?
"Every time I confronted God
with the reality I saw, he
became ugly. . . .
"You've got to understand
why I'm telling you all this
about myself. I want you to
see what sort of a poor human
being, what a bankrupt wretch
it is, who's sitting here before
you. I'm not a priest, I'm a
beggar who needs your help."

Life has an explanation.
What a relief.

Tomas: "Well, and what if God doesn't exist? What difference does it make?
"Life has an explanation. What a relief. And death—extinction . . . people's cruelty, their loneliness, their fear—everything becomes self-evident—transparent. Suffering is incomprehensible, so it needn't be explained.
"We've given gifts to each other, haven't we? You've given me your fear and I've given you a god I've killed." After Jonas leaves, Tomas looks out into the light.

God

Shot himself through the head.

desk; the vicar engages him in conversation, and when he asks the child whether he will come to confirmation class, is given a negative answer. Asked why, the boy simply mumbles, "I dunno." It is a minuscule scene, yet it leads Tomas further along toward loss of faith. When Märta returns with various kinds of medicine, there follows the finest scene of the film, about which Wood writes: "The schoolroom scene is, in its sense of human beings totally exposed to each other, raw-nerved and vulnerable, among the most painful and ugly in all Bergman (which is to say, in all cinema)." But the scene is not only painful and ugly; it is also extraordinarily moving.

The unloved, undesired woman's attempt to make this dour lover marry her, his weak excuses that her intelligence swiftly demolishes, his final malicious (but understandable) dumping of the truth in her lap are written with uncanny accuracy of psychological detail. Tomas runs through a catalogue of grievances against Märta, including her fussiness, nearsightedness, clumsiness, inept love-making, indigestion, eczema, menstrual disorders, chilblains, and ends up by accusing this unloved woman of aping his beloved dead wife. To which Märta replies with a terrible, deeply touching simplicity: "I didn't even know her." Tomas evades the issue: "I better go before I say something worse." And Märta, in a tone of dead calm, asks: "Is there anything worse?" The simple words combine with Ingrid Thulin's expression and inflection to make the moment one of the saddest and most beautiful in all cinema.

But Bergman is full of wonderful touches here: thus he makes Märta wrap the handkerchief she has been wiping her tears with around her thumb, and so stick it into her mouth as a kind of pacifier. Thulin magnificently portrays a quiet hysteria, a prolonged yet precarious balance on the edge of sobs. And in the midst of his attacks on her, Tomas is nevertheless allowed a moment of

Distraught because of his lack of communication with Jonas, Tomas breaks down in a coughing fit. As Märta tries to comfort him, the old woman appears at the church entrance and announces Jonas's suicide.

concern: "Stop rubbing your eyes like that!" But it is a rather me-·chanical concern, gruffly spoken. Again Märta breaks our heart with her answer: "Forgive me." The way Thulin twists her lower lip in pain could move stones, if not mountains.

More pathetic insistence from Märta, who persists in her contention that Tomas will go under without the ministrations of her love. Whereupon the vicar bursts out—"Why can't you shut up? Why can't you leave me be?"—and walks away toward the door. Märta is left in a curious posture: she has half slipped off her chair and, with her elbows on the small pupil's desk and her hands clutching the handkerchief like a rosary, she seems to be kneeling in a pew and fervently praying. The film takes a number of religious motifs—the state of being haloed, the *pietà,* immersion in prayer—and transposes them into a secular context. Finally, *Winter Light* will be seen as a religious myth, or myths, recast in secular, existentialist terms.

Now, as if in answer to her quasi-prayer, Märta obtains a proto-miracle: Tomas, who had already opened the door and started to leave without her, returns and asks—asks in a gray tone of voice, but asks nevertheless: "Want to come to Frostnäs with me? (*Pause*) I'll try not to be nasty." Stiffly, Märta inquires whether he means it, or whether he is merely in the grip of some new anxiety. "*Tomas:* Do as you wish, but I'm asking you to come. *Märta:* Of course, naturally I'll come. I haven't any choice, have I?" Every-

Tomas at the crossroads: the body is loaded into
a van, and he stands, now, totally without connection
in an indifferent world. (See Persona, *page 254,*
and The Clown's Evening, *page 60, for similar*
use of long shot.)

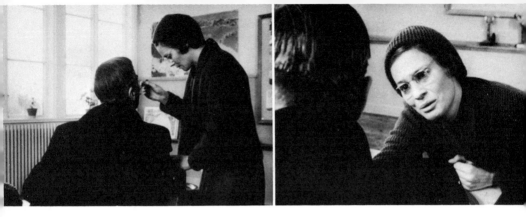

*In the schoolroom: Märta and Tomas begin truly
to learn about each other.*

thing in this scene works perfectly. Even the classroom background
contributes a wistfully ironic comment: here are innocent children's drawings on the wall (they are to recur, more bitterly ironi-
cal, in *Shame*); here, too, the boys' and girls' lavatory keys hang,
neatly labeled, peaceably side by side.

While Tomas waits for Märta, and just as he is about to get into
his car, a farmer goes by leading a horse. When he sees Tomas,
he takes his cap off to him. This small incident has fascinated me
each time I have seen the film—although, in all candor, I am not
quite sure what to make of it. For Robin Wood it is one of those
"cultural contradictions [that] form an unobtrusive background
throughout the film . . . a plough horse . . . led past [Tomas's]
large, smart car." But the car is neither that large nor that smart.
Rather, I think, the scene is meant to be a sobering irony: Tomas,
who has been unable to save a man from suicide, and has just
been beastly to his mistress (should a pastor have a mistress at
all?), is nevertheless saluted by this peasant out of blind respect
for his calling. The respect is for the cloth, and the man inside
must feel that he no longer deserves it. But if the man is not worthy
without the cloth, can the cloth be worthy without the man?

Tomas and Märta drive through the snowy landscape of the already darkening day. The overhanging trees reflect bizarrely in
the car's windshield and windows. The couple do not speak. Märta
waits in the car while Tomas goes to break the news to Mrs.
Persson. The Perssons, mother and three children, have just sat
down to dinner. Karin Persson comes out into the hall to meet the

184

minister, who tells her in the most colorless voice that her husband has shot himself. She sits down on the bottom stair, looks blankly ahead as she smoothes out her skirt, and says: "So I'm alone then." She refuses Tomas's offer to read something from the Bible together. As she is about to rejoin her children, and Tomas offers whatever help he can provide, she thanks him perfunctorily. Embarrassed, he says, "I spoke to him, but there was so little I could do." She looks at him from a great spiritual distance and says, "I'm sure you did what you could, sir," then goes back into the kitchen. There is a strong pathos of understatement —or, more exactly, unstatement—in this scene. Karin's last words carry a terrible indictment: either Tomas bungled the situation with Jonas, in which case the widow's words are a crushing irony; or he did the best that could be done, in which case how ludicrously inadequate a priest's best is! He watches, through the porch window, Karin brace herself against the edge of the table to tell the children.

The ride to Frostnäs continues silently. Märta is driving—so Tomas no longer refuses her help. At a railroad crossing, they must stop for a freight train to pass. The open freight cars carry industrial containers shaped like large coffins; the falling darkness makes them loom even more sinister. Here, in the screenplay, Bergman had Tomas relate a painful incident from his childhood. In the film, nothing of this—only the passing procession of mock coffins, and Tomas, seemingly out of nowhere, saying, "It was my parents who wanted me to go into the church." The image is po-

Go on, look.

As in many Bergman films,
their involvement leads them
to tear violently at, and finally
confront, each other. Similar
scenes in The Clown's Evening
(page 81) and Persona (pages
250 and 251) show Bergman
emphasizing an encounter
with the same use of light and
stark elemental composition.

You're all blurry

Can't you leave me alone.

Tomas for the first time
reaches out to someone. As
Märta sits in an attitude of
prayer, he turns from the
door to ask her to go with
him to Frostnäs.

As small a figure as on page 182 (see The Clown's Evening, *page 88), Tomas goes to break the news of Jonas's death to his widow.*

tently suggestive: the car waiting in front of the lowered boom, the train cluttering by with its symbols of death, and Tomas admitting to Märta, quite spontaneously, that he never had the vocation for the ministry. When the boom goes up and the car can proceed, it is as though an act of deliverance, or redemption, through confession—albeit secular confession—had taken place. Wood has rightly pointed out that this scene is no simple piece of symbolism; indeed, most of Bergman's alleged symbols do not represent one-for-one relationships; they tend, rather, to induce moods, suggest possible implications. Here it is as if what was blocking Tomas's life were both visually and verbally removed from him. He can go on to other things now.

As Tomas and Märta arrive inside Frostnäs church, Algot Frövik chatters away, apologizes for the bells' having rung twenty seconds too long, expatiates on his preference for candles in church ("electric lights disturb our spirit of reverence"), and, while blaming his wretched body's slowness, nimbly performs a number of preparatory tasks. Tomas sits down in the vestry to take off his boots and remembers to ask what Algot wanted to talk to him about. The hunchback relates how when his pains kept him from sleeping, he followed Tomas's advice to read something. So he read the gospels and found them veritable sleeping pills. But Christ's passion, that gave him something to think about. Algot has come to the conclusion that the physical torture could not have been the real passion; presumptuous as it may sound, he feels that he must have suffered as much as Christ, and for much

longer than the four hours of the crucifixion. As the amazed, occasionally nodding Tomas listens, Algot Frövik develops his theory.

The real passion of Christ was the agony of not being understood. At Gethsemane, his apostles had comprehended nothing;
Peter denied him, and they all ran. For three years Christ and the
apostles had lived together, and yet they grasped nothing. "Vicar,
that must have been a terrible suffering! To understand that no
one has understood you." As the camera keeps panning between
Algot and Tomas, the sexton observes that there was worse yet.
That was the moment when Jesus cried out believing that his
Father had abandoned him, and came to suspect that all his
preaching had been a lie. "Surely that must have been his most
monstrous suffering of all? I mean God's silence. Isn't that true,
Vicar?" And as Algot echoes Tomas's deepest concern, the camera
comes in tight on Tomas: his face is profoundly sad—he has to
look away, but he mutters, "Yes, yes." Christ himself has had to
endure the silence of both God and man. Who is this Algot? Peter
Cowie sees him as a sinister emissary of death, though Bergman,
as Cowie reports with disbelief, considers him an angel.

Meanwhile Blom, the organist, comes into the church, notices
Märta sitting in a pew, and goes up to her. He predicts that no one
will show up for the service, and, so far, he is right. He then starts
lecturing Märta about the worthlessness of her lover. He reminds
her that she is getting on and should leave Tomas and this dump
that "is in the grip of death and decay." He suggests that Tomas's
happy marriage was a fraud, though Bergman has cut from the

Tomas: "I spoke to him, but there was so little I
could do."
Mrs. Persson: "I'm sure you did what you could, sir."
One of Bergman's favorite compositions.
Tomas finds himself outside looking in. (See Persona,
page 257.)

film the lines in the screenplay that elaborated on this. Blom goes
on to make fun of the vicar's typical sermons on the theme of
"God is love, and love is God"—the very closing message of
Through a Glass Darkly, which Bergman here conclusively repudi-
ates.

Is there to be a service? The organist suggests to Tomas that
without worshipers there is no point in it. Frövik, consulted by
Tomas, gives no outright opinion but variously implies that he is
for it. He rings the service bells; they are supposed to make the
stragglers hasten. Still nobody. Märta is overcome with emotion
and kneels to pray: "If I could only lead him out of his emptiness,
away from his god of lies. If we could dare to show each other
some tenderness. If we could believe in a truth . . . If we could
believe . . ." Bergman first shoots Märta's head in profile. It is an
extraordinarily lovely shot: the lowered face is in darkness, and
only its outline is limned in light from a window. As Märta's voice
is heard finishing the prayer, the camera shows Tomas, his head
bent at exactly the same angle as Märta's, his fist close to but not
touching his brow, his face brightly illuminated by a lamp in front
of him and thus contrasting with Märta's.

Märta, the unbeliever, is the one who prays. Tomas, the minister, merely makes a fist. Märta is in darkness, yet tinged with light.
Her much greater certainty, her love, gives her only that narrow

edge of luminosity. Tomas, strongly lit, is still a man in darkness.
Or is he? The very fact that he is not praying may be a sign of his
awakening from a long, unsatisfactory dream. But Märta is praying. To whom? Surely not to that god of lies in whom she doesn't
believe? And yet she is in his church, praying in the posture that
goes with prayers to him. Moreover, as we know, she has prayed
before, and even, as it were, had her prayers answered. She is
praying for truth, certainty, a free giving of tenderness, and, curi-
ously, belief. But belief in what? And is Tomas, with his parallel
posture, asking for the same?

Algot Frövik inquires again whether there will be a service.
Tomas is uncertain. Algot says, "Well, of course, Miss Lundberg is
still here. And someone might still come in during the first hymn."
To his surprise, Tomas agrees. At Frövik's signal, Blom intones a
hymn, and Tomas, as Märta looks at him sadly, wonderingly, faces
his nonexistent congregation. His face is pale, and his expression
anxious. But this is not the frowning, dour, physically discomfited
face of the morning service at Mittsunda. And he is not wearing
his spectacles: it is as if his gaze were fixed on something farther
than glasses can reach. He speaks: "Holy, holy, holy, Lord God
Almighty! The whole earth is filled with his glory." An abrupt cut,
and the film is over. But what does this ending mean? And what,
then, is the meaning of the whole film?

It was my parents who wanted me to go into the church.

194

A Bergman journey: while Märta drives, Tomas looks deeply into himself. The car heads toward a railroad crossing.

Tomas: "It was my parents who wanted me to go into the church."

They wait as the train, with its coffinlike cargo, passes. The barriers are raised. They go on.

*Tomas and Märta at journey's end: Frostnäs, for
the evening service.*

One thing is clear: the end is a carrying on in spite of something
else. But what is being carried on? And exactly in spite of what?
There are essentially three ways of interpreting the ending: Christian, nihilist, and existentialist. The Christian view would be that
Pastor Ericsson, having gone through a series of trying experiences, finally realizes that even Christ had to endure his doubts
and despondency; fortified by Christ's example, he regains confidence and true faith, and proclaims God's glory and omnipres-
ence. The nihilist view would have the pastor lose his faith completely, and carry on without any hope, out of sheer cynicism—
simply because priesthood is his only profession, the easiest way
to go on earning a living. The existentialist view would be that
Ericsson, having through a number of jolts conclusively lost his
orthodox faith, nevertheless decides to carry on, taking God now
as a metaphor, a symbol for a new humanistic faith that might be
evolved. And he reconciles himself to the notion that uncertainty
and anxiety will have to be lived with, perhaps forever, but possibly shared with someone else.

The Christian view is represented by Arthur Gibson, who believes that "what Märta tells Tomas, God is persistently telling
man out of his great silence: 'You must learn to love,'" and that
Tomas finally realizes that God's silence is a sign of his trust in
man, his grant of supreme freedom, the silence and freedom being
synonymous. But there is no evidence for this in the film. Nowhere
in *Winter Light* are silence and love, or silence and freedom,
equated: there is no sense of trust or love coming from anything
but communication. When Märta and Tomas fight, words, even

wounding words, seem to bring them closer together. It is by telling him something that Frövik reaches Tomas and becomes, in Bergman's word, an angel. A self-made wall of silence dooms Jonas. And I cannot see how Tomas's preaching in an empty church, or the expression on his face in the last frame, could possibly suggest anything so joyous as fully renewed faith. Furthermore, there is Bergman's subsequent output to consider (in *The Silence,* for example, God, the sisters' father, dies), as well as his comment about *Winter Light* to Vilgot Sjöman (quoted by Cowie): "The three scenes outside the church, the vigil over Persson's body, the quarrel in the school room, and the visit to Persson's widow, are stages in the loss of . . . doctrinal faith."

But I think it is equally unsafe to take the totally nihilist position, as does Raymond Lefèvre (again quoted by Cowie), according to whom Tomas "plays his role with application. Like an artist who no longer believes in his art. Like a lover who caresses the woman he no longer loves." Stanley Kauffmann has a similar, though less extreme, interpretation: "The crisis is all the worse because it is a continuing one; nothing changes. [Tomas's] confession of spiritual vacuity does not alter his priesthood; he continues. Bergman seems to be saying that life was once lived in expectation of answers, now it is lived in continuity of questions. Crisis no longer leads to resolution." I myself, in *Private Screenings,* quoted the Swedish poet Gunnar Ekelöf to illuminate the film's ending: "It is its meaninglessness that gives life its meaning." But that is too bleak a view. Though a cynical nihilist might well carry on with his priesthood, he would surely not feel com-

Algot lights the candles, yet he also turns on the electric lights and the bells, which work by switch.

Christ's Passion, pastor.

Before the service, Algot, who is a hunchback,
finally gets to speak with the pastor.
Algot: "Christ's passion, Pastor. It's incorrect to
think of it as Christ's passion, isn't that so? We
think too much about the actual torture. . . . But
that can't have been so bad. Excuse me, it sounds
a bit presumptuous, of course, but physically, if I
may say so without being too assuming, I
must have suffered at least as much. . . .
"But think of Gethsemane, Pastor. For three years
Christ had been talking to these disciples. And
they hadn't understood a word he'd said. They
abandoned him, the whole lot. . . .

"But that wasn't the worst thing, even so! When
Christ had been nailed up on the cross and hung
there in his torment, he cried out: 'God, my God,
why hast thou forsaken me?' . . . He thought his
Father in Heaven had abandoned him. Surely that
must have been his most monstrous suffering of all?
I mean God's silence. Isn't that true, Vicar?"
Tomas: "Yes, yes."

Märta waits for the service to begin. Blom, the organist, arrives. He confronts her with a kind of lecherous disillusion, a disappointed man. He makes fun of her devotion to Tomas, and warns her of its consequences. Märta ignores him.
Blom to Märta: "That parson you're so sweet on. He's not much. . . .
" 'God is love, and love is God,' " he quotes sarcastically.

That person you're so sweet on, he's not up to much.

"Love is God"

"Love exists as something real."

If only we were sure

See Persona, *page 274.*

If only we believed...

So we hold the service?

The service goes on. . . .

pelled to continue to the extent of conducting services to empty
churches, or for the benefit of his unbelieving mistress. And,
again, the expression and intonation with which that consummate
actor Gunnar Björnstrand delivers Tomas's last words are not
those of a man to whom everything has become indifferent. It
seems to me that Bergman himself is Tomas, and that in this
work the film-maker is dramatizing the moment of his own loss of
faith, without having as yet evolved the anti-God attitude of a later
film like *Shame,* or the completely God-less world of *A Passion.*
Hence the aporia with which the film ends: an open ending, meant
to raise further questioning and doubt rather than provide hard
answers.

A slightly more hopeful interpretation, then, which I call existentialist, seems to me in order. We have seen how, in their various ways, Märta, Jonas, Algot (perhaps even Karin, by her patient
endurance) become Christ figures, as does, in his sense of abandonment, Tomas himself. In Algot's sermon to the vicar—for it is
hardly counseling that Algot seeks; at the utmost, confirmation—
Christ is revealed as yet another suffering human being. And, indeed, for all their Christlike features, Märta, Jonas, Karin, and
Algot are much more secular than religious figures: Märta is a
nonbeliever, Jonas a suicide, Karin refuses all religious help, and
Algot has the presumption to set his physical sufferings above
Christ's and to reinterpret Christ's passion. And if we are all
Christs, Christ is a symbol for something in us, just as God's si-
lence is really a metaphor for the winter light that prevails around
and inside us. I am inclined to agree with Robin Wood's reading

of this last scene: "The irony is very beautiful and touching, the disillusioned priest celebrating Vespers for the confirmed atheist, as a sort of inexplicit communion between them, using the traditional forms, which are all he knows, to express something not necessarily related to any orthodox Christianity."

What Tomas does become aware of in the course of the three hours depicted in *Winter Light* is general human aloneness and suffering, and the need to mitigate this through some sort of communion, or communication, some sort of sharing. Karin bitterly remarks that she is alone now, but goes in to share her grief with her children. Algot Frövik finds consolation in someone's—Jesus' —even greater aloneness; and also in sharing that insight with Tomas. It is no longer a question of love being God and vice versa, only, more modestly, of aloneness itself being sharable and so making life endurable, perhaps even an interesting journey. Seen in this light, the ending of the film is a heightened, more penetrating, less flamboyant version of the conclusion of that early film *Thirst,* an insight that, in one form or another, echoes through most of Bergman's work: hell together is better than hell alone.

Holy, holy, holy is the Lord
God almighty...

Bergman: "You know I was still convinced that God
was somewhere inside the human being, that he
had some answer to give us, and the end of the
picture was exactly that. You have to continue; if
God is silent you still have to go on with your work,
the service, without believing anything. Suddenly, one
day, God answers, but it's your duty to go on."

PERSONA

 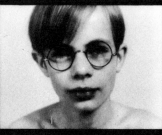

PERSONA

BIBI ANDERSSON 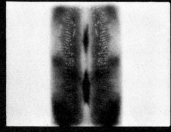 LIV ULLMANN

GUNNAR BJÖRNSTRAND  FOTOGRAF
SVEN NYKVIST f.s.f.

ARKITEKT
BIBI LINDSTRÖM  MASKER
BÖRJE LUNDH
ASSISTENT
TINA JOHANSSON

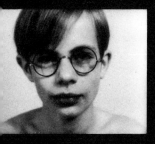  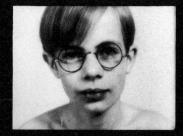

EN FILM AV
INGMAR BERGMAN

MARGARETHA KROOK

  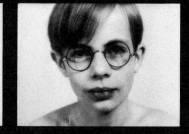

KLIPPNING:
ULLA RYGHE

KOSTYMER:
MAGO
ASSISTENT:
EIVOR KULLEBERG

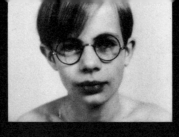
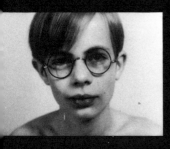

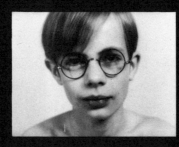

Bergman: *"I was in the hospital, the view out of the window was a chapel where they were carrying out the bodies of the dead, and I knew that house was full of dead people. Of course, I felt it inside me somewhere that the whole atmosphere was one of death, and I felt like that little boy. I was lying there, half dead, and suddenly I started to think of two faces, two intermingled faces, and that was the beginning, the place where it started."*

Persona is Ingmar Bergman's most difficult film; indeed, it is probably the most difficult film ever made. Difficulty in itself is not a virtue, of course; it may as easily prove empty pretentiousness, such as that of *Last Year at Marienbad*. But the difficulty of *Persona* is earned: earned by the seriousness, depth, innovativeness, and, finally, the uniqueness of the undertaking. *Persona*, I would say, is to film what *Ulysses* is to the novel: experiment raised to the level of calm assurance, radical individualism bending tradition toward itself, modernism becoming classical before our very eyes.

The basic plot is simple and sparse. A famous actress, Elisabet Vogler, married and the mother of a boy, elects suddenly to stop speaking. For months she has not uttered a word, but the woman psychiatrist at the hospital where the actress is being treated cannot find anything mentally or physically wrong with her. A young nurse, Alma, is assigned to care for Elisabet. The doctor has a

A blank screen. A line appears—the beginning. It turns into a door, through which a nurse emerges.

house by the sea to which she sends patient and nurse for a summer's cure: Alma's youthful warmth and solicitude should make Elisabet want to opt for renewed functioning. The summer house and its environs become the scene of a contest between the women—between the silence of the one and the chatter of the other—which goes from friendly to violent and bitter. In the telling of the story, dreams and reality become progressively more embroiled. In the end, Alma catches a bus back home by herself; the actress, too, seems to return to her acting, though this is not made quite explicit.

Several things greatly complicate this tale: (1) an elaborate framework of seemingly unrelated, or barely related, images at the beginning, end, and, briefly, in the middle of the film; (2) the manner in which the story is told, with sequences that can only be dreams, but without our being told where the dream begins or ends, or even who is dreaming; (3) the various ellipses or duplications, contradictory elements and unanswered questions; (4) the absence of an easily readable moral scale in the film: we are not given the usual clues to how justified or unjustified an action is, how good or bad the persons involved really are; (5) the loss of a sense of clear sanity in one world and insanity in the other: sanity, like morality, becomes an open question; and (6) the disorienting uncertainty about the sequence and duration of the various scenes, abolishing our sense of time.

The subject of *Persona,* as I see it, is a meditation on the numbers 1 and 2. It is a film about splitting and fusion, as Susan Sontag has noted; about one dividing into two, and two becoming

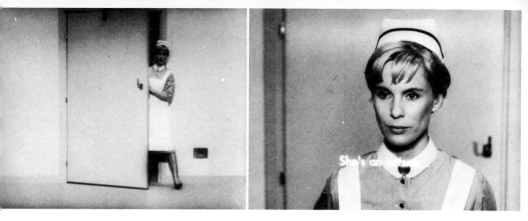

one. "The theme is that of *doubling;* the variations are those that follow from the leading possibilities of that theme (on both a formal and a psychological level) such as duplication, inversion, reciprocal exchange, unity and fission, and repetition. The action cannot be univocally paraphrased. It's correct to speak of *Persona* in terms of the fortunes of two characters named Elizabeth and Alma who are engaged in a desperate duel of identities. But it is equally pertinent to treat *Persona* as relating the duel between two mythical parts of a single self: the corrupted person who acts (Elizabeth) and the ingenuous soul (Alma) who founders in contact with corruption." *

The most commonplace aspect of the problem of 1 and 2 is, of course, the relation between a man and a woman. It is an early and basic *topos* of literature, as voiced, for example, by the Cavalier poet Sir John Suckling, "One is no number, till that two be one." But romantic love is the sole aspect of the 1 and the 2 that Bergman does not stress in his film: the principal characters of *Persona* are not lovers, for two reasons: first, because that relationship is so fundamental, traditional, emotionally charged that it would make all other aspects of the problem fade out of the picture; and, secondly, because hints of such a relationship between

* Susan Sontag, "Persona," in *Styles of Radical Will* (New York: Farrar, Straus & Giroux, 1968). This is the best treatment of the film in English thus far, although it does seem to me to err on a few important points of interpretation. It is also quite preposterous in the parallels it draws to other films and film-makers, and some of its facts are incorrect—thus it is not Alma who sucks Elisabet's blood, but vice versa. Nevertheless, it is a piece well worth reading and pondering.

The doctor tells of how Elisabet Vogler, the actress, went speechless in the middle of a play. Bergman uses various techniques to make the viewer participate directly in the film. Here he has us look over his nurse's shoulder, a frequent device of his. (See page 273.)

"For a moment she stopped dead."

She has been like this for three months...

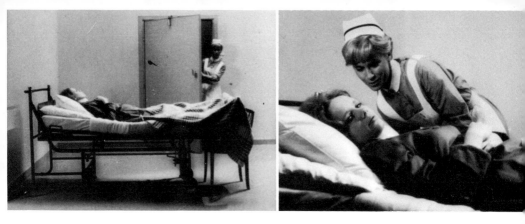

*Alma comes into Elisabet's
room. (See page 278.) Bergman holds a long take on
Elisabet's face—the face of
Elisabet Vogler the actress,
yet it is Liv Ullmann the
actress, a real woman, whose
celluloid image draws us in
as do Ingrid Thulin in* Winter
Light *(see page 172) and Bibi
Andersson in* A Passion.
*Over and over in this film
Bergman draws us into
the reality of what has been
recorded on film. (See pages
227, 259, and 286.)
Bergman: "I just want you to
sit down and look at the
human face. But if there is
too much going on in the background . . . the face is lost."*

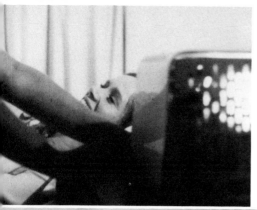

221

*The image fades into darkness as Elisabet falls
asleep listening to Bach on the radio. Bergman
has moved from light to dark.*

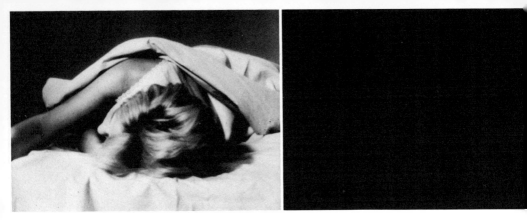

*Duality and oneness: the nurse cannot sleep, while
the patient sleeps calmly. Softly fading light, on the
one hand; black frames, on the other. States of mind
and being are shown in visual terms; visual technique
itself is the insight.*

the two women creep in anyhow, so that, if only subliminally, the
classic 1 and 2 do make their appearance.

To begin with, Alma and Elisabet stand for innocence and experience, the naïve and the *raffiné;* in a certain sense, perhaps,
even for body and mind. This duality can be embodied in two persons, as it is here, but it has a distinct relevance to the contradictory aspects of a single person. As complementary opposites, they
need and seek each other out following the principle of polarity;
but as conflicting, antithetical forces, they end up by clashing.
Consider the film's title. *Persona* is the Latin term for a mask, the
disguise by means of which an actor becomes a character—turns
into one of the *dramatis personae.* But in psychology (and Bergman was reading Jung at this time, and was, most likely, influenced
by him here) "persona" is the role a human being plays for the
benefit of other people, as well as to satisfy the expectations of
his own conscious self. Since Elisabet is an actress and Alma a
nurse in a psychiatric ward, both interpretations are plainly pointed
to. But "persona" finally means a person, an individual being, and
subsumes all the role-playing that goes into the drama of living.
Hence we are to see the film, first, as a dramatic conflict, a con-
struct, a movie; secondly, as a psychic contest between two people; and, thirdly, as the spiritual anatomy of a person or persons, a
study of interior human style.

But the three levels—dramatic, psychic, philosophic (or, if you

224

prefer, metaphysical)—can be viewed in another way. In that case, the conflict is, first, between acting and being, art and life, illusion and reality; secondly, between sickness and health, lies and truth, concealing and revealing; and, thirdly, between being and non-being, creation and destruction, life and death. And all of these things seen in a constant flux, a coming together and breaking apart, just as Alma and Elisabet experience and enact it in the episodes of the film that so intransigently resist coalescing into a single, simple story.

Persona, as has been variously pointed out, is one of those modern (or post-Mallarméan, post-Pirandellian) works of art that are concerned, at least partly, with themselves as works of art: with how they come into being, and what it means that they are, after all, works of art and not slices of life, and how this makes them superior or inferior, or both at once. Significantly, Bergman for some time did not allow stills from this film to be given out unless they showed the sprocket holes along one side, and the working title of *Persona* was, for a while, simply *Film.* The printed screen play is twice interrupted by speculations about the nature of film, and, as we shall see, the finished film, too, does a good deal to call attention to its filmness, much to the irritation of a critic like Vernon Young.

Persona begins with a set of disconnected images that Parker Tyler refers to as "a kind of amnion of visual irrationality." Am-

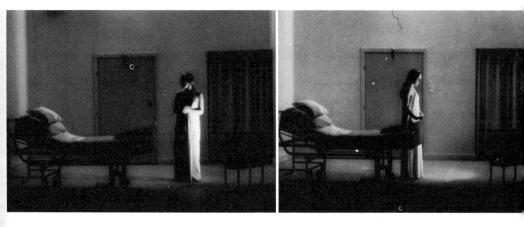

Elisabet is on stage in her hospital room. She watches television, and suddenly we are watching actual news footage.

Elisabet on film becomes as
real as the burning bonze
in the news.

Elisabet is back on stage—
backed into a corner. The
image of the bonze is back in
the television set, and we are
back as viewers.

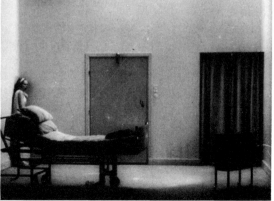

*Bergman shows time passing, like a scroll unrolling,
in a long horizontal tracking shot.
The scene is peaceful, bathed in shimmering light.
Wearing the same kind of hats, the women draw
close, in an atmosphere of intimacy.*

nion, certainly, but is it of irrationality? The film's first image is
darkness that turns into light, which proves to be the two carbons
of the arc lamp inside the projector. We now see the leader un-
furl, then images going by at almost bewildering speed. We observe a jerky cartoon of a fat woman in bathing attire washing her
hands, framed as if on a screen; next, occupying the entire screen,
we see "real" hands being washed. As Robin Wood puts it, "the
cartoon is shown as film, the hands as reality." Does this mean, as
Wood concludes, that "beside reality art is as crude as the jerky
movements of the cartoon beside . . . the real hands"? Or, simply, that we are going to see things from various points of view—
some stylized, some naturalistic—and that there is no one truth
about anything?

Next come bits from an old, silent comedy (or so it seems) in
which, again in jerky motion, a frightened man is trying to escape
from a skeleton and a devil that keep popping up before him. This
is actually a simulated silent farce that Bergman shot with some
Italian acrobats for his film *Prison.* In *Prison,* it represents part of
an innocent little film that Tomas and Birgitta-Carolina happily
project for themselves in their attic hide-out; in *Persona,* it seems
to serve a quite different, dual function. It stands for a primitive
stage of film-making, because these preliminary shots ontogeneti-
cally recapitulate the phylogeny of film. But, as several of us
pointed out in our original reviews of *Persona,* these shots may

also be emblematic of Bergman's previous cinematic output, of the main themes in his *oeuvre*. We see, next, a spider that may stand for the spider-God of *Through a Glass Darkly* and *Winter Light*. Then a hand rummages in the entrails of a dead sheep, followed by a knife heading for the animal's eye. This might, by prolepsis, prefigure *A Passion* (*The Passion of Anna*), in which a mad animal-killer is on the loose. The next shot is of one hand held down by another, while a nail is driven through the palm of the former. The reference might be to *The Seventh Seal* and its peripatetic penitents, one of whom, in fact, represents the crucifixion; or it may be an allusion to the young witch in the film, who is broken on a kind of cross and burned.

There follows a brick wall that dissolves into a landscape of wintry woods; then a spiked iron fence around an old building and snowbanks in front of the fence. One could perhaps see some reference here to *Winter Light,* though it is safer to interpret these shots as images of harshness and sterility in general, from which we go to shots of an old man and woman stretched out, apparently dead, on hospital beds—we must be in some sort of morgue. We hear the sound of something dripping—water? formaldehyde?— also distant voices and doors slamming. There is much hovering of the camera over these two corpses, and over a third one, that of a young boy (Jörgen Lindström)—the son from *The Silence.* After various close-ups of hands and feet, there is one of the old

Intimacy increases. Bergman moves in on it,
placing Alma and Elisabet indoors, in one of his
alternations between inside and outside, light
and dark. Using lighting from a direct source, he
creates high contrast, so that the identically clad
white figures of the women stand out strongly in
the dark room, and all concentration is thus
directed toward them.
Actively involving the viewer: the camera moves
increasingly close to Alma confessing her seduction and Elisabet listening priestesslike, until the
viewer becomes absorbed, and images rising from
Alma's words form in the viewer's mind and
superimpose themselves on the images on the
screen.

The women come together.
The space is ambiguous, as
is the happening. States of
being merge. Where does
dreaming end and waking
begin? (See pages 223, 225,
260, 263, 279, 281.)

woman's face seen upside down as it hangs over the head of the bed. At this point, eerily, her eyes open—a shot that will be echoed importantly on two later occasions. The boy is now awakened by the ringing of a telephone (*The Silence* began with the boy waking up in a train compartment); he tries crawling back under his sheet or shroud and assuming a fetal position, but cannot get back to sleep, death, or the womb. Finally he puts on his glasses, picks up a book, opens it at a marked page, and starts to read. It is the same book this boy was reading in *The Silence:* Lermontov's *A Hero of Our Time.* The boy looks up from his book at us and stretches out his hand toward us. There is a reverse shot, and he is now seen caressing a wall, or screen, or translucent plate glass on which a woman's face, of huge size, keeps dimly fluctuating in and out of focus. The woman's eyes, under the boy's caresses, open and close. We notice now that it is not one face but two: an almost imperceptible shuttling between the visages of Alma and Elisabet. (So, too, the boy in *The Silence* put his hand to the train window, to stare through it at us, the audience.) Then the titles of *Persona* start coming on.

There is a shot that appears a little after the titles, but belongs, in a sense, with this pre-title sequence, and that I want to discuss here: a dark-haired woman in Grecian attire is playing a scene from some Greek tragedy. She is silent, dazzled, or stunned. Although she is on a stage, with stage make-up and lighting, we can see her being photographed by a movie camera behind which are the cinematographer and director, *i.e.,* Sven Nykvist and Ingmar Bergman. We are told by the off-screen voice of the psychiatrist that this is Elisabet Vogler, the actress, with a black wig, as Electra. And Stanley Kauffmann has gone on to speculate that the "disjointed beginning, made of splinters of horror and showmanship, is like a quick jagged tour of the actress's mind—images that terrify and also, in an Olympian way, amuse her." * It seems to me that there are numerous signs pointing to this prologue's taking place in the author's, rather than in the actress's, mind, as I have already suggested.

It should be stressed that Mrs. Vogler's Electra was played on the stage, but the Electra we see is both on stage and in the movie being shot by Bergman. The black wig, moreover, is not strictly necessary to the role; it is probably meant to recall the black wig worn by the hero of *The Face* (*The Magician*) for his impersona-

* *Figures of Light* (New York: Harper & Row, 1971).

Back in documentary reality, surface reality: Bergman returns the viewer to the reality of being a viewer, of the film being a film, of the actress being human.
Elisabet pops up from space beyond the frame and takes a picture of you. (See page 286.)

*Now the viewer becomes voyeur, through an objec-
tive long shot placing us in the bushes spying. We
are drawn into the action with a zoom.
Alma has read a letter in which Elisabet speaks of
her as interesting to study. Brooding, she retaliates,
leaving a sliver from a broken glass in barefoot
Elisabet's path.*

tion or skulduggery; and his name, too, was Vogler. The prologue
is plainly self-referential. Thus Bergman conceived *Persona* while
he was hospitalized with Ménière's disease, an affliction of the
inner ear, causing, among other things, vertigo and loss of equilibrium. That could, to some extent, explain the film's spatial oddi-
ties, symbolized, as it were, by a number of heads shown hanging
over the edge of the bed and seeing the world, accordingly, upside
down.

The building next to his hospital room, Bergman has said,
housed the morgue, whose whereabouts the hospital authorities
tried to keep hidden from the patients, denying even its very existence. Hence, presumably, these corpses that might not be corpses.
More important, though, they stand for the *dramatis personae*
whom the author, in Pirandellian fashion, summons from non-
being into being. The boy must surely be an image of Bergman
himself, a hero of our time, forbidden the luxury of crawling back
into the womb of non-existence. Even the fact that he must put
on glasses for reading suggests Bergman's current state of irritation at having to wear spectacles. That Bergman will speak of
himself as a child we see confirmed in his Erasmus Prize acceptance speech, "A Snakeskin Filled with Ants," which serves as
introduction to the script of *Persona,* where we read: "With a

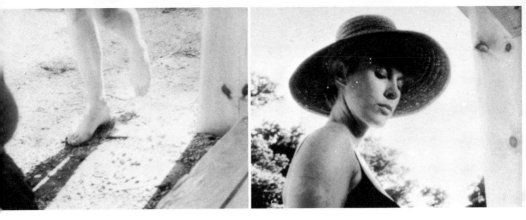

child's repressed hunger, I threw myself into my medium. . . ."
That the boy's condition in this prologue, between death and life,
sleep and waking, is Bergman's view of his and our lives, is confirmed by his remark in an interview with Nils Petter Sundgren:
"The reality we experience today is in fact as absurd, as horrible,
and as obtrusive as our dreams. We are as defenseless before it
as we are in our dreams. And one is strongly aware, I think, that
there are no boundaries between dream and reality today" (quoted
in Cowie's *Sweden 2*).

The boy Bergman, then, is seen at the evanescent frontier between reality and dream as he reaches out for contact with us,
the audience; but the gesture is then translated into a reaching
for the shifting, elusive face on the wall. That dual, duple face is,
of course, what *Persona* is about, and the boy-Bergman accom-
plishes three things with his gesture. He is guiding us toward his
work, the film; he is suggesting, both by reaching for us and by
the semitransparency of that wall, that he and his tale are aiming
at something beyond: at life, at us—*de te fabula narrat*. And,
thirdly, we are given a sense of the bewilderment, the puzzlement
of the boy before the strange, dreamlike transformations of the
image in front of him: woman, who is both Alma and Elisabet,

239

*Alma goes inside to await
the result. Pain. They regard each other through
the curtained window, Alma
inside, Elisabet outside.
The surface of their intimacy has begun to crack
and burn, as—suddenly—
does the film . . .*

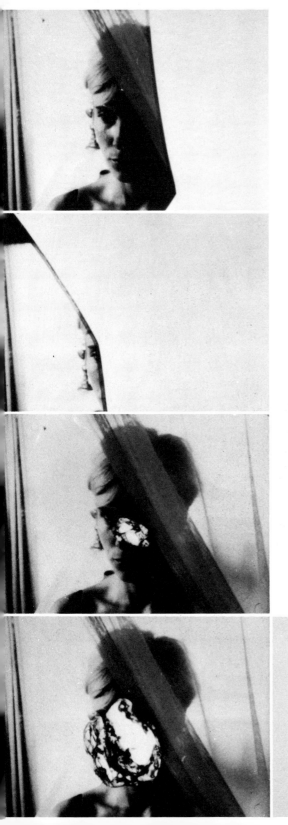

and as Alma's face burns
away, we see images of
what lies beneath.

handmaiden and dominatrix, and who ultimately cannot be grasped.

The themes of the two and the one, and of the merging of dream and reality, are present from the beginning. Out of the two burning carbons of the arc lamp comes the single light that illumines the film. The sequence of brief, harsh, disjointed shots suggests dream but may be reality. Finally, the dual image at which the boy gazes is the first of many to suggest that Alma and Elisabet flow into each other without quite becoming united: the eternal attraction-repulsion of the two who never fully merge.

Next we see the film's credits interspersed with brief, almost subliminal shots of images from the film. Most of these are recognizable and, subsequently, relatable to the film, *e.g.,* the rocks along the seashore where Elisabet and Alma will be staying, or a Buddhist monk immolating himself with fire, a scene Elisabet will watch on TV. It is, in Bergman's lovely phrase to me, "the film's impatience to get started." But there are also a few mysterious images here. One is an erect penis (now excised from American prints, presumably by United Artists), which, I suppose, signifies the erotic incident from Alma's past. There is also a less easily decipherable image—at least given the speed at which it goes by. This proves to be a woman's lips, slightly parted, in extreme close-up, and shown vertically rather than horizontally. This may, again, have to do with the upside-down view of things, but, more likely, is meant to suggest the vagina, a perpendicular mouth. It may also refer to the printed screen play, which contains an act of oral intercourse; more probably, it is a metaphoric conflation of sex and the word, the creative and the procreative, the mind and the flesh. Even more puzzling is an image of reticulations, almost completely inscrutable even on the Movieola: it might be of twigs

The film began with some of
these images (see pages
211, 214). Here, as though
latent, they seem to break
through from beneath the
surface of the film.
When the film begins to rip
with Alma's torment, it
dissolves her face. She was
looking out through the
curtains. Now, as the camera
gradually refocuses, the
shadowy figure looking out
the window sharpens and
becomes Elisabet.

246

Elisabet's face then dissolves in light.
Her body appears to be part of the hills
behind her. She touches Alma's face.
The women are together, yet apart.
While Elisabet wears the same straw
hat as earlier (page 231), Alma does
not. Alma looks increasingly boyish.
The light is full of contrast, the background harsh. Alma gets no response
to her questions.

Alma flies into a rage, ac-
cusing Elisabet of using her.
She is screaming at a
statue of a female.
She forces involvement on
Elisabet.

You did, because it wasn't sealed.

The gathering storm of violence explodes. Bergman shoots Alma and Elisabet in close-up against a wooden wall. There is nothing to distract attention from the characters. The happening is stripped bare. It is elemental. Bergman uses the wall much as he used the light on page 232.

In Shame, *Bergman also used such a wooden wall as the only background for an act of explosive violence, which again comes as the ultimate confrontation after a slow build-up of tensions between two characters. (See page 272.)*

No, don't!

...e you something you won't...

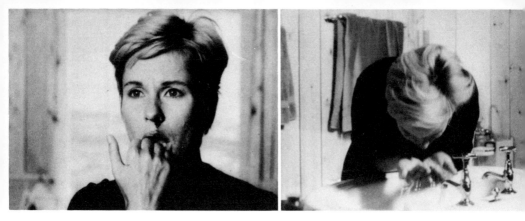

In the bathroom: Alma washes away the blood. (See hands washing on page 211.) There is pain and guilt. Did she bring it on herself? What has she inflicted?

shown in negative exposure, or it might be the veins in the human eye in extreme close-up.

After the titles we get a white-out (the white of the eye?) which turns into the white wall of the psychiatrist's office with a white door in it. The film thus begins, so to speak, *ex nihilo,* with Alma stepping through that door. The woman psychiatrist is a curious figure: knowing yet somehow repellent of aspect; perceptive, but in some smug way repulsive about it. (Perhaps that is the way some psychiatrists are, come to think of it.) She explains Elisabet Vogler's case to the nurse, and here the film gives us an illustrative flashback, the shot of Elisabet's sudden silence while acting Electra, a shot we have already discussed. We hear, along with Alma, about that momentary silence, a fit of laughter later that evening, and the prolonged, continuing mutism that followed. Alma accepts the assignment to take care of the actress, and goes in to see her. She tells her about her humble origins, her age, her mother's having been a nurse. Mrs. Vogler listens, smiles, and says nothing. Alma goes back to the doctor and expresses her doubts about her suitability for the task. She explains that to embrace mutism willfully requires great mental powers with which she, Alma, might not be able to cope. She seems to sense that there will be a battle of wits, endurance, strength, and that she might lose. But, in the end, she accepts the challenge of the assignment.

Alma is tending Mrs. Vogler. It is dusk. The light in the bare hospital room is less harsh than usual. The nurse turns on the radio, which is broadcasting a play, some sort of romantic drama.

A woman's rather histrionic voice is asking, "What do you know about mercy?" and Elisabet bursts out laughing. This must be the same sort of outburst of laughter as the one she had after her last performance in *Electra.* But the scene is more explicit in the published screenplay. There the female voice on the radio is accorded three highly rhetorical utterances. First: "Forgive me, forgive me, my love, oh, you must forgive me after all! Forgive me and I can breathe again—live." Then: "What do you know of mercy, what do you know of a mother's suffering, a woman's bleeding pain?" Finally: "Oh God, you who are out there somewhere in the dark that surrounds us all, have pity on me. You who is love . . ." In both printed screen play and film the actress then laughingly turns off the radio. Mrs. Vogler is rejecting what seem to her melodramatic outbursts about love, maternity, and God. She herself has cast off all such feelings by her withdrawal into muteness. In either version, screenplay or film, the gesture of refusal is plain, but it is not quite clear whether the actress's rejection is aimed at the feelings themselves, or at the theatre's aping them, or at theatre as a whole.

Alma admits that she doesn't know much about theatre but thinks it "enormously important, especially for people with problems." This, obviously, is a layman's, and particularly a therapeutically oriented layman's view, and it further arouses the actress. She has lost her faith in the moral-therapeutical value of her work. But now Alma turns on another station, and we hear some Bach chamber music. Elisabet listens raptly and seems transfigured by the sounds; in fact, she seems on the verge of speaking. Outside, the day is sinking, and her face gradually darkens, though it remains lit up from within, as it were. (Sven Nykvist, the cinematographer, is performing his customary miracles.) We know that Bergman loves Bach and music in general, and it seems reasonable to assume that the mistrust of the word expressed in *Persona* by so many diverse means is deliberately contrasted with this trust in music. Does some art, then, have a therapeutic value after all? I would call this scene, with its ambiguities, a key scene—except that *Persona* is made with such absolute economy that every scene in it is a key scene. The implication here, if I am interpreting correctly, is that art cannot attack the most deep-seated problems frontally, as the radio play would, but only by indirection, insinuation, abstraction, as Bach's music does.

The next scene shows Alma's unrest. She is trying to sleep in

A long horizontal track, like that on page 230, but
now the women are tiny running figures in a limitless
space. The chase ends in confrontation.
Alma: "Please forgive me."
When Elisabet can't answer, only observe, Alma is
left with the comfort of the earth and the stones.

I want you to forgive me.

Dusk: outside, Alma is cradled by the rocks; inside,
almost a votive figure—yet menacing, Elisabet lights
the lamp.
Elisabet goes out, comes back in. Alma's changed
face shows us how far we have come.

her little room, but keeps switching the light on nervously, then
turning it as impatiently off again. Visually, this jerky shuttling
between a bright light and pitch darkness contrasts significantly
with the dark that slowly gathered around the actress in the
previous scene: it is a fine example of the changing rhythms that
make a film come alive. And it also conveys in eloquent images
the different ways in which the two women feel: the one slowly
immersing herself in her emotion, the other, once the surface
equanimity is broken, wildly oscillating between bright, rather
forced cheerfulness and dark engulfment. Alma tells herself about
her forthcoming marriage to her boy friend, Karl-Henrik, and the
children they will have. That and her job give her a tremendous
sense of security—or so she mutters. She then wonders about
what is really wrong with the actress, but not about what ails
insomniac Sister Alma.

Elisabet's hospital room again: dim light, coming mostly from
the television set the actress is watching. The composition and
lighting of this shot are admirable: soft, mysterious chiaroscuro;
texture and shadows on Elisabet's nightgown sensually stressed;
a luminescence along the walls; two darker areas (a door, a cup-
board) framing Elisabet. The TV documentary is about Vietnam
and in English, and the narrator's portentous intonation is, in its
way, as specious as the declamatory tones of the radio actress.

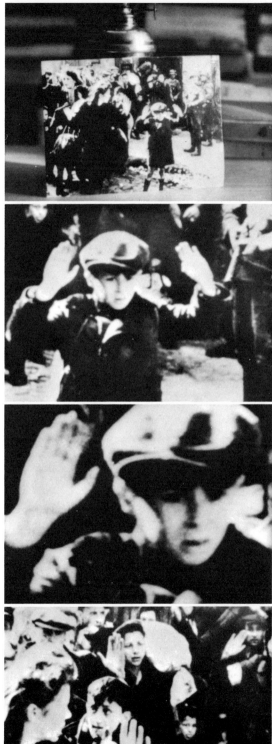

Elisabet prayerfully contemplates a photograph. As with the televised burning bonze on page 227, Bergman suddenly confronts Elisabet and us with an image of human suffering drawn from real life—the Warsaw Ghetto, an anguished woman and a frightened boy.
Elisabet, too, has a boy who is suffering—at her hands. The reality of Warsaw, Elisabet's reality, and our own merge.

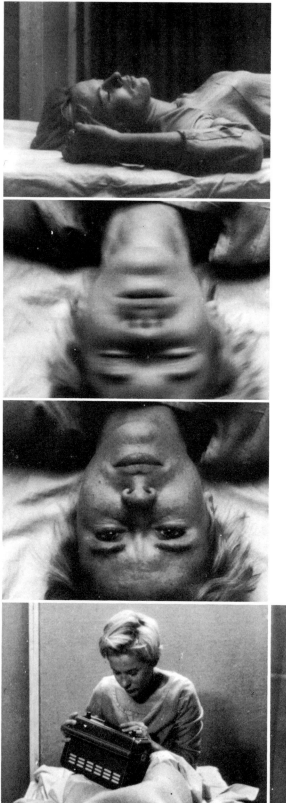

Sleeping-waking. See pages 210, the old woman, 211, the boy.

We cut back and forth between the TV screen and Elisabet, and there are contrasting movements: on the TV screen, people are rushing toward the bonze who has set himself on fire and is, agonizingly slowly (Bergman stretches the duration by repeating the image), burning to death. In the hospital room, Elisabet is horrifiedly backing away farther and farther from the television set, until she ends up in a corner, like an animal at bay. Her hand goes up to her face, and she lets out the ghastly sound of a cornered animal, something halfway between a scream and a moan. Is it the world—in the form of war and death—that is too much with her? Or does she recognize in the bonze's self-immolation a more explicit form of her own mutism and abdication?

In the next scene, Alma reads Mrs. Vogler a letter from her husband. The women have reached a genuine understanding, so that Alma interprets Elisabet's nods and expressions, and can crudely communicate with her. The actress even trusts the nurse enough to let her read out loud this very personal letter. And Bibi Andersson is marvelous as she reads, her nursely efficiency somewhat shaken by the intensity of the words, her reading sometimes faltering because of the struggle with the handwriting. The husband's letter is a rather pathetic attempt at reaching Elisabet, and is not very different in style from the radio play she turned off. "You taught me," Mr. Vogler writes, "that we must look at each other like two anxious children full of good will and the best intentions but governed by powers that we can barely control." The actress has been getting more and more panicky as Alma continues: "Do you remember you said all that? We were out walking together in the woods, and you stopped and held on to my coat belt?" At this point, Elisabet snatches the letter from her.

Alma then hands Elisabet a snapshot that was enclosed in the

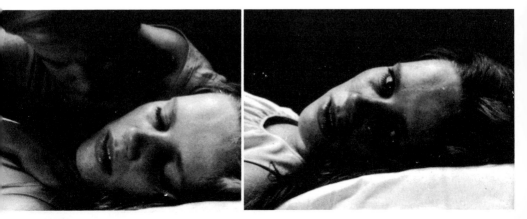

Elisabet's "blind" husband appears. He speaks to
Alma as though she were Elisabet.

*He makes love to Alma as though to Elisabet.
Bergman's lighting has begun the process of
merging the two identities that culminates on
page 271.*

letter. It is a picture of the actress's son. "He looks terribly sweet,"
Alma says, and Elisabet looks at the photo for a long time, then
tears it in two. She clearly wants no emotional holds on herself,
and particularly resents being reminded of her own former de-
pendency. There is something striking about her tearing the picture only once, however, lengthwise. She apparently cannot bear
to destroy it utterly; and the split down the middle is symbolic not
only of her hostility toward the child but also of her own duality;
moreover, it fits into the pattern of halvings and doublings that
characterizes the film. The musical background for this tearing
of the snapshot, by the way, is much the same as for the scene
in the prologue when the boy was watching the twofold feminine
face fluctuating before him.

The next scene, in which the patient and nurse are sent by the
woman psychiatrist to her own summer house by the sea, is a good
example of how Bergman abridges his scenario, leaving in the
film only what is essential. Thus he cuts from the movie a number of explanatory remarks of the doctor's, concentrating instead
on her big speech; this, too, he makes more concise and, by minor
rewording, more pointed. The doctor tells the actress that she
understands her anguish: the gulf between being and seeming; the
fear of being exposed in one's nakedness, but also the hunger to
expose oneself, to be seen through. The lie that is in every gesture,
the grimace in every smile (on stage? in life? or both?). Suicide
is too crude, so one opts out by way of silence and catatonia: no

more play-acting, lies, wrong gestures. "But reality is diabolical. Your hiding place isn't watertight. [The doctor seems almost malignly triumphant here.] Life trickles in from the outside and you are forced to react. [This trickling in of life, was that the sound of dripping we heard in the morgue as the corpses started coming alive?] Nobody asks if it is true or false, whether you're genuine or a sham. Such things matter only in the theatre, and hardly even there." This is the horrible truth: life is more mendacious than the theatre, mere carrying-on will suffice in it. It is not all that important to be true in one's acting; it doesn't matter at all in one's living. The two opposites, theatre and life, have become one in their joint untruthfulness, their common unimportance.

The doctor continues about Mrs. Vogler's mute passivity: "I understand and admire. You should go on with this part until it is played out, until it loses interest for you. Then you can leave it, as you left all your other parts, one by one." This is the psychiatrist's master stroke. She has now equated Elisabet's refusal to act, on stage or in life, with yet another piece of acting. To strip off all one's personas is to assume yet another persona. And the doctor's (the world's?) acceptance of this essentially antisocial strategy as "admirable" but also ephemeral, something one will get bored with, shows the sinister power of the powers that be to admire, accept, absorb, and so disarm the individual who turns against them.

An extreme long shot of the women disporting themselves in the woods is accompanied by—for the first and last time in the film—

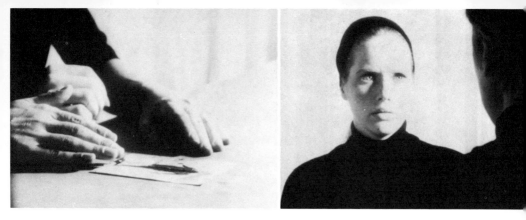

Elisabet has matched the two halves of the photo-
graph of her son, which she had torn. She tries to
cover the picture; Alma uncovers it.
Alma speaks Elisabet's mind about her son.

narration. The voice is that of Bergman himself; he may have got
the idea for doing his own narration from Godard. In any case,
the device serves the purpose of distanciation: we are reminded
of the presence of the director, of film-making, lest this seaside
setting draw us overmuch into a mood of romance, storytelling,
escape. It also serves as foreshortening, for by it Bergman tele-
scopes a series of repeated summer activities that bring the two
women closer together. We now see them after a mushrooming
expedition, sorting out and peeling the edible mushrooms at an
outdoor table. They are humming a tune in unison—a form of
communication, even if not speech—and they are wearing clothes
that are rather similar and emphasize the resemblance between
the wearers. Yet at this stage Alma is still reverently keeping her
distance from the actress she admires—refusing, for example, to
have her palm compared to Elisabet's. Both women have on broad-
brimmed straw hats that some critics have compared to those worn
by Vietnamese peasants. Perhaps, indeed, we are to be alerted to
the fact that bloody wars are fought on various scales, even on
tiny, seemingly harmless ones such as these skirmishings.

In another scene, lying on the rocky beach, Alma reads a passage from a book about man's abandonment on earth, and about
our hopes for salvation in another world being, just like our doubt,
only proofs of our anguish, of our unconscious sense of that
abandonment. Alma asks Elisabet whether she believes this; the
actress, with a curious Gioconda smile, nods assent. The nurse

*The previous scene is re-
peated exactly, but this time
with the camera focused on
Alma's face rather than on
Elisabet's. This repetition
shows two identities sharing
the same consciousness in
one happening in time.*

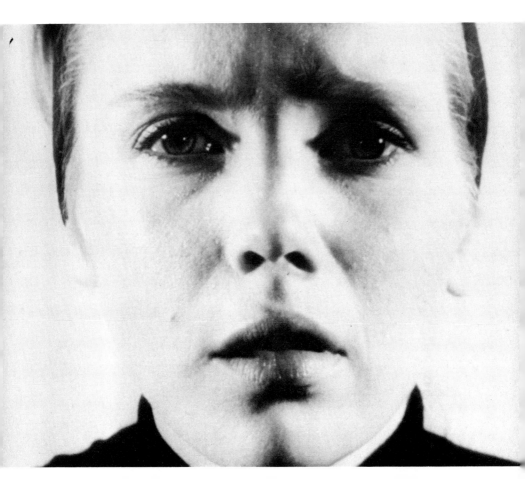

Complete mergence: Bergman makes manifest in one visual image the insights contained in all the preceding scenes.

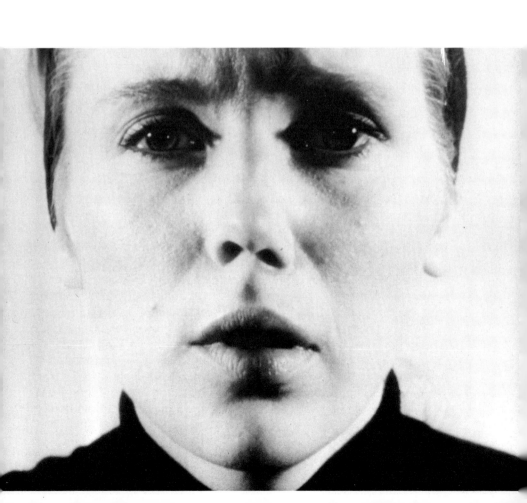

*We go back to images we have already seen in
different contexts. Bergman constantly rearranges
the same images to show the various faces of reality.*

says she cannot accept such things. The rest of the film will proceed precisely to shake her faith, and bring her, at least in her
dreams if not in her waking, to a total loss of positive beliefs. As
an example of Bergman's tact, let me mention that the screenplay sets this scene in a drifting motorboat, a rather too obvious
symbol. The film places it on the shore, but a rocky, pebbly shore
that enhances the grim thought without resorting to visual over-
explicitness.

Rain, in the next shot, has driven the women indoors. Alma is
indulging in relaxed chitchat, little confidences that the actress
encourages in various silent ways. Among other things, Alma tells
about an old-age home exclusively for retired nurses that is right
next to her hospital. She expresses her veneration for these totally
dedicated women who lived for their work and die in little rooms
still close to it. She wants to believe in something so strongly as to
offer up her whole life to it. But unlike those nurses, always in
uniform, she is already out of it. In fact, Elisabet and she are wearing ever more similar clothes; in this scene, plain black dresses
which, in juxtaposition, make it hard to tell where one woman
ends and the other begins. There is, for instance, one shot where
Elisabet's body and Alma's head seem to be joined together so as
to fashion one person. At another moment, the women seem to
share one dark body from which emerge their two pale heads.

Somewhat under the influence of liquor, Alma now tells the
actress about her private life, love affairs, sexual experiences. The
narrative is introduced by a typical gesture that we see Alma make

frequently: smoothing her short blond hair back from her forehead. It is a gesture Bergman may have found in Godard's *La Chinoise,* where Juliet Berto keeps making it. But there it is nothing more than a tic; here, we shall see, it acquires a special significance. Alma tells about the married man whose mistress she was for five youthful years. He tired of her, but he was that first love, the real one, she says, that cannot be forgotten—a quaint combination, this, of the sordid and the romantic, but typical of the kind of glossing over that Alma practices. Yet she now admits, under the actress's somewhat quizzical gaze, that it was *"en riktig novell"* —a veritable (dime) novelette.

Alma is egged on by Elisabet's attentiveness: no one has ever paid such attention to her. She tells about her fondness for Karl-Henrik, her fiancé; but "you love only once," referring, of course, to the married man. Still, she is faithful to Karl-Henrik. And yet . . . She drinks a little more, smoothes her hair back from her brow: there was that time on the beach. The gesture takes on, in context, a mildly autoerotic character. She and a voluptuous girl named Katarina were sun-bathing nude on an isolated beach. Elisàbet listens, stretched out on the bed, and smiles encouragingly, enticingly. Alma is curled up in a chair opposite her. Again, according to the script, "she strokes a non-existent curl from her forehead." And she goes on to tell of the two boys on the cliffs above the sun bathers, skulking about and stalking them. The girls remained defiantly uncovered, and the boys, emboldened, came closer. One was sixteen, perhaps; the other, barely fourteen.

273

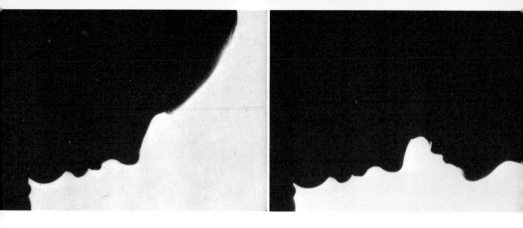

Another aspect of mergence, this time not per-sonified, as on page 271, but abstract.

Elisabet listens, immobile and fascinated. Alma fumbles for a cigarette and shakily lights it. There follows an account of an intense little orgy, in which all sorts of sexuality were enacted with innocent, untrammeled lust on the boys' part, and only slightly more knowing carnality on the part of the girls, especially Katarina. As the narrative progresses, we become aware of several things. The girls were, in a sense, performing for each other, Katarina seducing Alma, and each increasing her sexual appetites by watching the other. Alma says that they were both wearing those large straw hats—the very hats Alma and Elisabet have been wearing in the present. So the Alma-Katarina sexual identification is transferred in our minds to the Alma-Elisabet relationship. The fact that the nurse and actress are wearing similar clothes and, later, similar nightgowns, heightens the sense of an involvement, a relation. The actress lies on the bed, as if absorbing the narrated sexual experiences into her own body; meanwhile, Alma's fidgeting about, getting up and moving around the room, faintly suggests the activity of the male partner in intercourse. This, however, does not mean that she dominates the actress—any more than those two inexperienced boys on the beach dominated the women lying under them. But Bergman is trying to suggest apartness as well as fusion between the actress and nurse. Thus he frames Alma with the contours of a large, canopied fireplace in the middle of

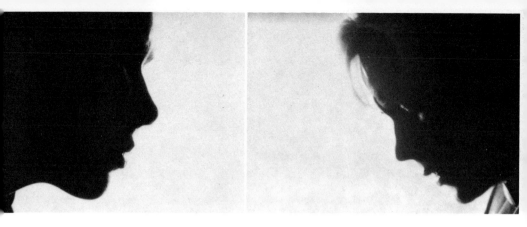

the room, through which he shoots the nurse. The effect is rather like a Francis Bacon portrait, with the sitter framed by the outlines of a prism—the mere suggestion of a cage that he could walk through, but that isolates him nevertheless. Moreover, Bergman conveys the sheer lust of the incident not through flashbacks, an easy device he rejects, but through such things as the tone of voice Bibi Andersson was able to muster—a "tone of shameful lust" that Bergman was surprised and delighted by. The shameful lust, Wood cogently adds, is there also in the way Alma crouches in the chair. We are, in his words, in "a context of human complexities."

There is, then, to quote Susan Sontag, "a charged, trancelike . . . contact between the two women." Even Pauline Kael, in her generally unsympathetic and, I think, imperceptive review of *Persona,* concedes that this "almost fierce reverie [is] one of the rare, truly erotic sequences on film [and] demonstrates what *can* be done on screen with told material." * Once again, this scene resumes the motif of the two and the one, but in a more complex way: when two pairs are having intercourse in the past, and one pair is reliving the incident in the present, who becomes one with whom? Ironies within ironies: on the night after the beach orgy, Alma and Karl-Henrik had the best sex they ever had together; but when Alma proved pregnant, there had to be an abortion. Would the child have been the product of the beach, or of that supreme love-night with the fiancé?

* *Kiss Kiss Bang Bang* (Boston: Little, Brown and Co., 1968).

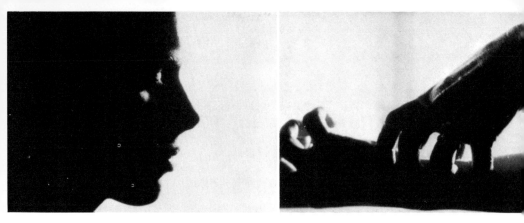

*Alma yields her arm to Elisabet. But then she in turn
inflicts severe punishment. (See page 250 and
Bergman on page 32.)*

By the time Alma is telling these things to Elisabet, it is quite late at night. The nurse bursts into sobs. She clearly has strong guilt feelings about that abortion. In the screen play, she now asks tearfully: "Can one be entirely different people, right next to   , at the same time?" Where I left a blank, the text reads *vartannat,* which is mysterious. We expect "each other," for which the correct Swedish word would be *varandra; vartannat* is the neuter form, and applies to things rather than people. Unless this is simply a slip of the pen or a compositor's error, it is baffling. In any case, the film changes this to: "Can you be one and the same person? I mean two people?" This *cri de coeur* of Alma's fairly summarizes the whole film: can two people become one? But, under emotional stress, Alma expresses herself badly, and her wording is significant: can one person even be a consistent whole and not split into two or more people?

Now the problem of twoness and oneness becomes more prominent. It is no longer a question of Karl-Henrik and Alma but of Alma and Elisabet. Sitting at the table across from the actress, the nurse remarks on their being look-alikes. Though, she concedes, the actress is much more beautiful, she, Alma, could change herself, at least internally, into Elisabet, if she tried very hard. "You," she goes on, "could change yourself into me just like that! [Snaps her fingers.] You have much too big a soul, though. It would stick out all over." The subject of one being's possession by another has been broached. As she talks on, Alma is becoming sleepier and sleepier. A voice—it is Elisabet's—says: "You must go to bed

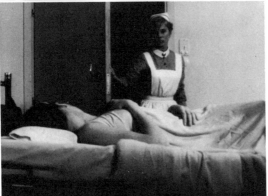

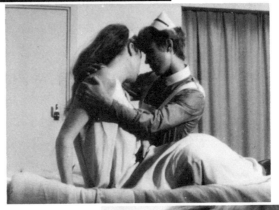

278

*All the events, the levels of
consciousness, are contained
in the fullness of the moment.
(See pages 218, 219 and 220.)
Alma brings Elisabet to speak.
She says "Nothing," as her
face . . .*

Nothing.

*fades into the persisting
Elisabet-Alma image.
We are shown another level of
consciousness, and again
Alma awakens.*

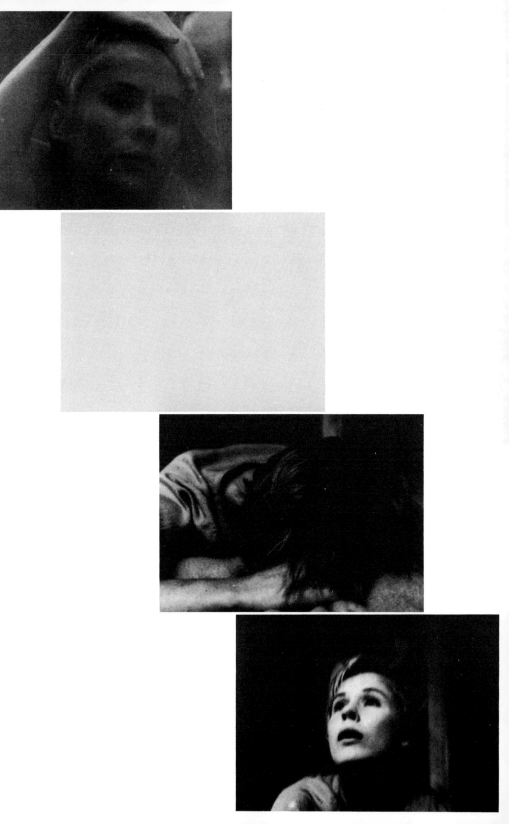

The persistent image: as Alma
looks in the mirror, smoothing
back her hair, the vision of
Elisabet doing the same is
superimposed. Their hands
blend into one.
Though Alma's mirror image
is of her separate self, Alma-
Elisabet is there as well.

The moment, continuing to expand (see page 218)
as it has throughout the film, goes on
timelessly. (See Bergman on page 32.)

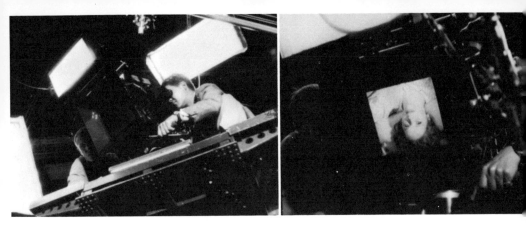

The moment includes those
who made the film—Bergman,
Sven Nykvist, Liv Ullmann—
as it also includes the burning
bonze and the woman and
child in Warsaw.
Liv Ullmann is Elisabet, back
at work. Her upside-down
image recalls Alma on page
260 and the old lady on
page 210.

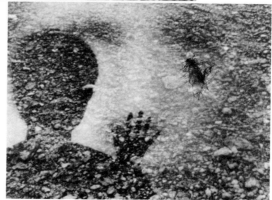

Like the little boy, we and
Bergman, Alma and Elisabet
reach out to feel the human
image.
Bergman: "You sit in a dark room
and you have this little bright,
bright square before you and
you just sit there and look at its
movements every moment and
you never move your eye. And of
course, it goes right inside you
and right down in your emotional
mind—in your unconscious."

now, or you'll fall asleep at the table." Alma rouses herself and repeats: "I must go to bed at once, or I'll fall asleep at the table." Has Elisabet really spoken? Or did Alma merely dream it?

Bergman, as we know from *The Face* (*The Magician*) and *Hour of the Wolf,* was considerably influenced by the German romantic novelist and storyteller E. T. A. Hoffmann. In Hoffmann's novel *The Devil's Elixirs* (1815–1816), Count Viktorin and the monk Medardus, who unbeknown to each other are half-brothers, are perfect look-alikes. The entire novel is preoccupied with one of Hoffmann's favorite themes, that of the *Doppelgänger,* or double, and that of a protagonist whose actions are decreed by a strange, external power. Viktorin sometimes voices Medardus's thoughts, while Medardus believes that his own deepest speculations are being verbalized by a voice outside himself, although it must be he himself who is speaking. Whether or not Bergman got the idea from Hoffmann, the fact remains that the spiritual fusion of the two women is now well under way.

There follows a night scene, beautifully staged and photographed. Alma has fallen asleep in her bed. It must be near dawn; foghorns can be heard outside. Alma's room looks somehow different: there seem to be more doors than necessary, and gauzy curtains everywhere. Through the billowing gauze curtains, herself wearing a sheer and rippling nightgown, Elisabet appears. She moves like a sleepwalker, and disappears through another curtained door. Almost immediately, she returns. Alma has, or seems to have, awaked; she goes to Elisabet and puts her head on the actress's shoulder. Their very similar nightgowns touch and, as it were, merge into one large wave of chiffon. From behind, Elisabet gently strokes Alma's hair. This we recognize as the equivalent of Alma's own frequent gesture, complete with erotic overtones. Autoeroticism has yielded now to real eroticism for two players. Elisabet then caresses her own hair: she not only merges with Alma by caressing Alma's hair; she also becomes, by caressing her own, another Alma, becomes Alma herself. Then she slowly bends her head down toward Alma's shoulder. Is she merely repeating Alma's gesture reciprocally? Or is she about to go beyond that, and kiss Alma's shoulder? Or is she really aiming for the neck and at something sharper, deeper than a kiss? There are publicity stills extant showing Elisabet avidly gluing her open mouth to Alma's neck. In the film, Bergman lets the image dissolve before we get to anything so explicit.

It is morning now, on the beach. A gray day. Elisabet's head suddenly pops up, a camera held to the eye; seemingly, the actress is photographing us in the audience. The nurse is now revealed standing far to the back of her. Bergman is trying to draw us into the film again, indicating that the action depicts us as much as the characters in the fable. Alma inquires whether Elisabet spoke to her the night before. The actress gives a slight shake of her head. And did Elisabet come to Alma's room last night? Same slight headshake. We wonder: is Elisabet lying, or did Alma dream or imagine it all? Truth and untruth, reality and dream are becoming hard to tell apart. Are they, in fact, separate things, or just the two faces of one?

It is a rainy day and Elisabet is finishing some letters. Outside the window, Alma pulls up in a car (a car never to reappear in the film—is this a mistake?) and offers to post the actress's letters along with her own. She is driving through the wet landscape now; it has stopped raining; but there is still a dribble from overhanging branches, and large drops roll down the car windows. A letter from Elisabet to her doctor lies on the seat next to Alma; it is unsealed. Did Elisabet leave it so deliberately? Accidentally? Or, as the Freudians might have it, with a fortuitousness concealing an unconscious intention? Alma cannot resist; she stops the car and begins to read. Among other things, Elisabet writes that Alma is spoiling her and seems, in an innocent way, a bit infatuated with her. She tells of enjoying studying the nurse, of encouraging her to talk. The letter casually mentions the orgy, and the nurse's complaint "that her ideas don't tally with her actions." (A case, presumably, of the one splitting into two halves.) She confesses, in short, to using the nurse, and enjoying it. Alma reads with growing agitation and brief, stunned interruptions. On the sound track, we hear the same sounds of water dripping as in the morgue sequence. Shakily, Alma steps out of the car, and we now see her standing, in her shiny black raincoat that reflects the light, before a pond in a clearing of the woods. At her feet, in the leaf-speckled, slightly wavy water, Alma's image is blurry, as if in the process of dissolution. It is a lovely, odd, somewhat posed shot, but it suggests all the more a state of unease, isolation, not knowing where to turn. Even one's reflection, that usually comforting double, seems to be treacherously deserting.

There follows Alma's vengeance, a brilliantly directed scene. Sitting in her bathing suit on a bench just outside the house, Alma accidentally knocks over an empty glass. She sweeps up the pieces, but decides to leave a big, jagged one right in the middle of the path: Elisabet is walking about, also wearing a bathing suit, and barefoot. Alma watches. Elisabet moves to and fro along the path, carrying out her breakfast things, but her feet keep missing the splinter. The women are not talking to each other, but now Alma's silent, hateful watchfulness speaks as loudly as ever Elisabet's silence did. The nurse finally goes into the house, disappointed, as it seems. She continues looking out through the window. Finally, from off screen, comes a sharp cry of pain. Alma looks both exultant and anguished through those gauzy curtains; Elisabet glowers back. Now, at mid-point, we see the film break inside the projector and begin to go up in flames. The devil and skeleton from the farce sequence pop up again, followed by the hand with a nail through it, an eye in extreme close-up, then the white of the eye alone with the network of tiny veins crisscrossing it. Then, out of focus and very hazily, Elisabet puttering around the house, drawing curtains open, etcetera. At last, the film slowly gets back into focus.

What has happened? The film has ripped and burned from the weight and heat of emotion it was unable to bear. But why such self-destructive violence over a mere piece of broken glass and a cut foot? Bergman has staged this scene with insidious suspense and a formidable impact of understated, implied hatred. A small wound from a tiny weapon manages to carry the implication of total warfare between two individuals. But to understand these implications fully, we must now consider the real identities of Alma and Elisabet. The names provide clues. Alma, in Latin, means fair or kindly girl, and the nurse is, indeed, all blond generosity. I doubt if Bergman is aware of the word's Celtic meaning, "all good," but he is surely cognizant of the Spanish one, "soul." The name Elisabet comes from the Hebrew and means "consecrated to God." Now the only god the actress is consecrated to is her art, and, to some extent, she must be taken (despite Bergman's caveat) as an image of the artist. But she is also obstinately dedicated to herself, her own truth, so that she is also a sort of divine egomaniac. Needless to say, the pursuit of art and egomania are hardly mutually exclusive. Alma, then, is the simple soul who cares for the artist, and on whom the artist leans and battens. Yet it is not a simplistic relationship in which the nurse is all good and the actress pure selfishness. The artist and concerned layman mutually sustain and exploit each other.

Nevertheless, to the good soul, it is a terrible shock to discover, first, that her façade of service to others, to Elisabet, has cracked; and that, furthermore, her very attempts at identification with the actress have been rejected. Thus both her sane, modest, official view of herself and her secret and grandiose one have been proved false. She had, in Vernon Young's words, imagined "Elisabet coming to her in the night, i.e., being touched by art." * Yet she has been revealed a mere entertainment, at the utmost a subject for study, as far as Elisabet is concerned. But the actress must feel equally enraged: this little, unimportant nurse, whom no one had ever listened to, and to whom she has been a steady, devoted, distinguished audience, giving ear to mediocre babble—this creature should dare turn against her, physically assault her? And, to come back to Alma again: she must be horrified at having not only forgotten to heal, but also actually injured a patient entrusted to her care.

Significantly, when the film disintegrates under the burning pressure of so much hatred and self-hatred, it must reconstitute itself by recapitulating some of the images from its beginning, and requires time and effort to get back into focus. Elisabet now settles down outside the house in a deck chair and reads a play by Shakespeare. Alma remarks (they have, apparently, made up to an extent) that if she is reading plays, Elisabet will soon be well; then they'll both be able to leave. But she gets no response, or a negative one. Alma begins to break down: she pleads with Mrs. Vogler to speak about anything—the weather, tonight's dinner, the temperature of the water. Or even just read aloud from her book—as a personal favor to her. The nurse cannot stand the silence any longer: her own words, by themselves, seem so inadequate. She chides the actress for having made it easy for herself with her mutism, and again begs her to speak. The words, clearly, would not need to have any great meaning, and in most talk they indeed have very little—only this: they are a symbol of community. Alma, close to tears, rebukes Elisabet: "I always thought that great artists experienced other people through a lofty feeling of compassion. That they created out of compassion, the need to help. How stupid of me!" She has been dancing a ballet of rage around Elisabet's deck chair; the actress looks at her with a mixture of amazement and anxiety. The nurse, the simple consumer of art—which, as she earlier said, she considered therapeutic—who believed in the

* Cinema Borealis: Ingmar Bergman and the Swedish Ethos (New York: David Lewis, 1971).

kindness of the artist, finds out otherwise. She becomes hysterical and accuses Elisabet of having used her and thrown her away. Then she turns against herself and makes fun of her own melodramatics. All the time, she keeps nervously putting on and removing her very dark sunglasses. Finally, she tosses them down on the terrace floor, then collapses herself. She accuses the actress of having drawn out secrets from her, and made fun of her behind her back. And all this just to use her, presumably, for some future role. She becomes incoherent: "You can't. You can't." We are witnessing, after the questioning of the value of words, the very breakdown of speech. Silence at one end, gibberish at the other, and never shall the twain be one.

Alma rants, and tries to force Elisabet to speak by twisting her arm. The actress tears herself away, and hits her face so hard that the nurse staggers. But she rushes back into the fray and spits into the actress's face. Elisabet slaps her again, hard, and the nurse's nose starts to bleed. Enraged, Alma spots a boiling pot of water on a hot plate; she grabs it and goes for the actress's face with it. Elisabet recoils and cries out: "No! Don't!" Alma stops, bleeding all over her lip, but malignly triumphant. And in terrible, half-shrieked words, she rubs it in: she has made the actress afraid, after all. Not, mind you, made her speak; made her *afraid.* She starts for the actress again, but is stopped cold by Elisabet's laughter. Bitterly, Alma observes that *she* cannot just laugh things away. The scene is superbly choreographed: Alma's stalking dance around Elisabet's immobility—one against one—yields to a crazed outburst of the two women intertwined in a grim ballet of physical violence—two in one, but a one that is fighting itself. It all leads up to Elisabet's detached, derisive laughter: the very thing Bergman describes in the "Snakeskin" speech as "art is free, shameless, irresponsible."

After washing up, calming down, and accepting some coffee from Elisabet, Alma tries suasion once again. Must speech be honest and truthful, she asks; need life be free from quibbling and making excuses? "Isn't it better to be silly, lax, babbling and lying? Don't you think one improves a little even by letting oneself be as one is?" What Alma presents here is, though simplistically expressed, a not uninteresting notion: that in our lies, our machinations, our sloppiness is our truth; that by yielding to them we become more ourselves and, in a sense, better. At length, she blurts out her deadliest assault: "People like you can't be reached. I wonder whether your madness isn't the worst kind. You act healthy—so well that everyone believes you. Everyone but me. Because I know how rotten you are." This is the attack on the artist's morality, his very sanity, that is made in some form or other in almost all of Bergman's later films (and some of the earlier ones), stated here with the most lucid concision.

It would seem, then, that once the ordinary human being gets to know the artist intimately, from the inside, the result cannot be anything but resentment, hatred, contempt. But the next scene, a kind of spiritual reverse pan, promptly gives us the other face of the coin. Now we are outdoors rather than indoors: against the cozy interior of the cottage, the home truths of the good little nurse may have seemed supremely convincing; but against the austere, elemental coastline, the harshness of whose crags already emblematized cold metaphysical truths, Alma's pieties appear diminished. Contritely, she is running after Elisabet. A magnificent tracking shot follows the actress running away as the nurse, over wounding rocks and through lacerating bushes, pursues her with her apologies, losing ground and also her patience. It appears that it is because of Alma's love and need for her that Elisabet must forgive her; but the actress, unresponsive, rushes on. Alma hurls herself on the rocks and cries in fury and dejection, suddenly aware of a hierarchy, real or imagined, entitling the actress not to deign to forgive her, "because it's not necessary." And, once again, her words, in rage and despair, lapse into incoherence: "I shall not . . . That I shall not . . ." Another shot, later on, shows her sitting quietly and somberly on the rocks, as darkness descends. Inside, meanwhile, Mrs. Vogler finds between the pages of a book a famous photograph: women and children of the Warsaw ghetto being hustled off to their deaths by Nazi soldiers; the center of attention is a little boy, pathetically holding his hands up. The actress seems transfixed by the picture, around which her eyes wander. She is presumably reminded of her son. Does it require the sufferings of an alien child and the mediation of the camera to make her remember the anguish of her own little boy? Or is the point of the scene to connect the torment of the people in the film with the general misery of the world?

There follows a sequence of scenes that are no longer real in any sense of the word. They are dreams or hallucinations, and they seem to be preponderantly Alma's. But we cannot be quite sure. At times, the point of view appears to shift to Elisabet's, or it may be a fusion of points of view: as if a nightmare or phantasmagoria were shared by Alma and Elisabet, united in their tortured visions. We see Alma asleep, in a position reminiscent of those dead bodies in the prologue. She now seems to want to wake up, but cannot raise her head and has a hysterical fit that could be either a dream or waking. Her head hangs down over the head of the bed, just like the old woman's head in the morgue. Is a sleeper about to wake? A dead woman about to come to life? A girl blind in her waking about to see the truth at last in the more penetrating illumination of dreams?

The bedside radio is spouting disconnected phrases, interrupted by static: ". . . doesn't talk, doesn't listen, cannot understand . . . What means to use to make people listen? . . ." This may be Alma's mind lamenting its failure to reach Elisabet, but it also echoes that earlier scene in which the highly emotional radio drama provoked Elisabet's contemptuous laughter. Radio, a prime medium of verbal communication, here seems to go berserk and to bemoan the lack of communication. From outside, very far away, a man's voice calls, "Elisabet!" The nurse gets up to scrutinize the sleeping actress, and has her little moment of exultation: she can now see all the tiny blemishes and marks of mortality that the sleeper cannot conceal: wrinkles, puffinesses, scars. The man's voice calls again outside the window, and Alma walks out into the night toward it.

The camera now shows Elisabet following Alma. The man in the garden is Mr. Vogler; his sudden emergence from the dark frightens the nurse. He is wearing very dark glasses, like those of a blind man. Is he truly blind? Or just blinded by passion? Or are the glasses merely a projection of Alma's own very dark sunglasses: do we all want to soften—indeed, to hide from—the harsh glare of truth? But dark glasses at night? Behind Alma we now see Mrs. Vogler, smiling ironically. Vogler proceeds to talk to Alma intimately: about love, about being together, about their son. Obviously, he takes her to be his wife. She tells him that she is not Elisabet, but he does not seem to hear any better than he sees. Elisabet herself then guides Alma's hesitant hand toward Vogler's anxious face. The action now shifts to Alma's bed, where she and Vogler have been making love. But Bergman shoots from Elisabet's bed, a few feet away; with her face turned toward us, the actress is listening to the love-making, to the tendernesses being exchanged. Is this *her* dream now? Or is Alma dreaming a suffering

Elisabet into her dream of revenge? The camera's positioning and, earlier, Elisabet's gently putting Alma's hand to Vogler's face would tend to dispute such an interpretation. Vogler is unsure of himself; Alma soothes him by telling him what a marvelous lover he is. What is being re-enacted here, albeit with a difference, is Alma's youthful seaside orgy. By sharing Elisabet's huband right in front of her, Alma is getting closer to, almost making love to, Elisabet—just as on that beach she and Katarina were vicariously enjoying each other through those inexperienced, almost object-like, boys. Most revealingly, Vogler says to Alma that they should "take each other for children. Tormented, helpless, lonely children." Though this may suggest the boy in the morgue, it is more palpably an echo of Vogler's letter to his wife, which Alma read aloud to her: "You have taught me that we must look at each other like two anxious children. . . ." The dream is rehashing and fusing fragments of reality, and improving on it: Alma, impersonating Elisabet, acts out the devoted wife and mother (she sends her little boy a loving message and a present by proxy). In other ways, however, the dream is worse than reality: Alma is torturing Elisabet with all this lovey-dovey stuff, and the actress's face in the foreground is visibly anguished. When, in the end, Alma bursts into a tirade of self-hatred, is she speaking for Elisabet, or for herself, or for both of them?

The two have, however tormentingly, become one through a third party. A third party who is, at least figuratively, blind, and thus reduced to playing a passive, subordinate role.* Now the fusion is about to become more direct. In the next sequence, Alma catches Elisabet looking at the picture of her son. The actress has somehow joined the torn halves of the picture into one, and the nurse joins her in gazing at the photo. Alma now launches into a lengthy monologue in which she relates and analyzes the steps that led to Elisabet's becoming a mother, and to her subsequent rejection of her child. As the camera focuses on Mrs. Vogler's appalled, guilty reactions, Alma, seen from the back or not at all, goes through a detailed account of how the actress was challenged by a provocative remark—about her having everything in the world except motherhood—into getting pregnant. She soon

* Vernon Young (*Cinema Borealis,* pp. 224–237) offers a rather fanciful interpretation of *Persona,* in the course of which he suggests that Vogler is the Theatre, a cast-off mistress, wooing Elisabet-Bergman back to itself. I find this explication, to put it mildly, unconvincing; Bergman is not an allegorist.

regrets it, tries every way of aborting the baby, fails; she hates the infant, is tempted to strangle him but cannot do it. She nurses the baby with disgust, farms him out to relatives, escapes back to her professional life as a great actress. But the boy develops an incomprehensible passion for his mother, whose frigid indifference he rewards with love. The more she finds him weak, homely, distasteful, the more he approaches her with dewy, adoring eyes. Her conscience torments her, and she grows afraid.

The camera now reverses its point of view and focuses on Alma as she goes through the same monologue once again, exactly as before. But now, instead of watching Elisabet cringe, we observe Alma rubbing it all in with intense *Schadenfreude.* Again we hear the self-same dismal recital, accompanied by agonized musical underscoring, and then—suddenly—we realize that something has happened to Alma's face in close-up: it is bisected longitudinally, and one half of it is—Elisabet. Yet this has not come about unprepared for. Earlier during this sequence, sharp chiaroscuro halved Alma's face into hemispheres of light and darkness, looking almost like two separate faces. And, unless my eyes play tricks on me, Bergman has, albeit subliminally, sneaked part of Liv Ullmann's face into Bibi Andersson's before; then, at the words "You think he's repulsive, and you're afraid," the grafting becomes manifest. It is a disturbing and painful image, precisely because the two women do look somewhat alike. (Bergman said he got the idea for *Persona* from seeing Liv Ullmann in a Danish-Norwegian co-production, *Short Is the Summer,* based on Knut Hamsun's *Pan,* and being struck by her resemblance to Bibi Andersson.) As a result, the two half-faces do not look merely like disparate, unrelated forms arbitrarily juxtaposed; rather, they look like one face, but a sick, monstrous face that does not quite hang together—that contradicts itself, wants to split apart, is struggling against an enforced oneness. It is as terrible as seeing an object—a lamp, a table, a painting—straining to disintegrate; as if the atoms constituting our everyday reality suddenly became visible, only to start flying off in different directions. But what makes the image particularly distressing is that, for quite a while, you are not fully aware of what is happening, and the face before you only conveys a kind of agony no face on screen has ever conveyed before. An agony without symptoms you are used to and can comprehend, such as a gaping mouth, eyes torn open, twitching nostrils, and whatnot.

This scene has generally been interpreted as a projection of the nurse's sick fantasies and guilt feelings about the abortion she once had upon the actress, to whom she attributes her own pangs of conscience. How else, runs the argument, could Alma know what really happened, why the actress got pregnant, had the baby, felt as she did, and so forth? She wasn't there, and Mrs. Vogler certainly didn't tell her anything. But for this simple, essentially unimaginative nurse to come up with a case history so detailed, so psychoanalytically acute, and one that cannot, in all fairness, be interpreted as a mere projection of her own guilt (after all, what she is talking about here is not an abortion but its opposite: having a baby, and the miseries resulting from it)—that, to me, seems equally impossible, wholly beyond her inventive powers. Of course, the scene is, if it is to be interpreted logically at all, a dream, a fantasy, a vision. In a dream, the average person may conjure up imaginative constructs beyond his waking abilities; also, the nurse may be familiar with case histories similar to Elisabet's and can perhaps extrapolate from them. Nevertheless, the fact that we are given this scene twice, from two different angles, indicates that Bergman must attach special importance to it; he must see it as more than just a nurse's self-indulgent fantasy or hallucination. True, this may be the very sequence Bergman had in mind when he wrote, in the liminal paragraph of the screen play, "On many points I am unsure, and in one instance, at least, I know nothing." I myself firmly believe, though, that just as the faces of the women merge here, so do the minds behind the faces, and that the scene (or two scenes, or two in one) represents the combined consciousness, and subconscious, of both women.

At this point, it may be useful to consider what must have been one of Bergman's sources for *Persona:* Strindberg's short one-act play *The Stronger.* This *quart d'heure* deals with a battle of wits between two actresses, Mrs. X. and Miss Y., during which only the former speaks, while the other contents herself with a proud silence and various, often condescending, facial expressions. In the course of the brief play, Mrs. X. figures out that Miss Y. has been her husband's mistress, and that, indirectly, she has been imposing her tastes on the household of Mrs. X. and her family life. Mrs. X. now resolves to go home, make passionate love to her husband, and take matters into her own hands. The curious thing, however, is that though critics of *Persona* have called attention to the borrowing from *The Stronger,* they have misinterpreted the

play. In *The Stronger,* according to Vernon Young, "a psychological duel between two women reveals that the one who remains
silent is the stronger of the two. . . ." Susan Sontag describes
The Stronger as "a duel between two people, one of whom is ag-
gressively silent." In *Persona,* she writes, "as in the Strindberg, the
one who talks, who spills her soul, turns out to be weaker. . . ."
But is this so open and shut a case? Strindberg himself wrote out
some instructions for his wife, Siri, who was about to create the
part of Mrs. X. on the stage. Analyzing the character, he explained:
"She is the stronger, i.e., the softer. What is hard and stiff breaks,
what is elastic gives and returns to its shape." And here is Martin
Lamm, perhaps the leading Swedish Strindberg scholar: "In a
passage intended for the preface of *Miss Julie,* Strindberg had
spoken about 'thought transference.' In *The Stronger,* he obviously
tried to produce a kind of inner communication between Mrs. X.
and her adversary. Mrs. X. reads Miss Y.'s thoughts, but at the
same time she feels Miss Y. is inducing her to express everything
she is thinking. 'You've sat there staring and winding all these
thoughts out of me like raw silk from a cocoon—thoughts, perhaps
suspicions.' She discovers that Miss Y. is a vampire: 'Your soul
crept into mine like a worm into an apple, eating and eating, boring and boring, till there was nothing left but the skin and a little
black mold.' But suddenly Mrs. X. becomes aware that she herself
is 'the stronger' and that Miss Y.'s silence is not an evidence of
strength—it only means that she has nothing to say." Lamm then
adduces the playwright's letter to his wife that I have just quoted,
and comes to this conclusion: "Nevertheless, even with this commentary, it is difficult to be convinced of this talkative woman's
superiority in this battle of the brains." *

Precisely. *The Stronger* is a problem play, and one cannot be
sure which of the two women really is the stronger. And so it is in
Persona, too. What is especially relevant to the film is Strindberg's
notion of "thought transference," heralded in *Persona* by that in-
struction to go to bed and avoid falling asleep at the table, of
which one cannot be certain who said it. Now in the repeated
monologue sequence of *Persona,* Bergman goes beyond thought
transference into "being transference"; not just thoughts or words,
but the very essences of two persons have become fused. Robin
Wood has put it plausibly: "Bergman needs a means of finding a

* *August Strindberg* (Rev. Ed. 1948), Harry G. Carlson, trans. (New York: Ben-
jamin Blom, 1971), p. 226.

dramatic approximation for inner states of breakdown, disintegration and merging—at once the loss of identity and a kind of universal extension of identity. What we see on the screen is to be taken as interchangeable—as happening within (or beneath?) either woman's consciousness or both, an expression in action of experiences taking place below the level of action." And, significantly, Strindberg's suggestion of vampirism in *The Stronger* will now appear more explicitly in *Persona.*

There follows a scene in which Alma and Elisabet are standing in the living room, their faces continuing to stalk, confront, cover each other. Alma is now wearing her nurse's uniform again, which she did not do in any of the preceding seaside scenes. She accosts the actress once more and, according to the script, "hears this voice that speaks on and on with her own voice." She begins seemingly rationally: "I don't feel like you, I don't think like you, I'm not you." She then comes to the verge of truths too bitter for her: "I'd like to have—I love—I haven't," and promptly deviates into nonsense. "Say defend nothing . . . Cut a light . . . A sort of another . . ." So begins a series of frantic, incoherent phrases. We hear things like "A desperate perhaps," of which we can make something. But then, again, "Takes, oh yes, but where is nearest . . . It's called what-no, no—us—we—no—I . . . Many words and then nausea . . . incredible pain . . . the throw!"

Two things, nevertheless, are clearly conveyed: the theme of confused, exchanged identity; and a sense of words not being able to cope with the psychic stress that pushes them out, with the feelings they are meant to express. There are marvelous, compelling images in this scene, dredged up from below the decipherable layers of the psyche. Thus Alma, in her uniform, sits at a table and, in a frenzied rhythm, bangs her hands and forearms on it, turning her palms now up, now down. There are extraordinary camera angles and croppings of heads: so both women are seen in a tight shot, their faces in shadow and tilted downward, Elisabet's lowered profile cutting off all but the chin and mouth of Alma's similarly downward-tilted profile bending toward Elisabet, and just behind her. From Alma's open mouth—in which, in back lighting, we can see even a strand of saliva—poisonous words pour forth. Below the faces, there is only dazzling light, as if they were hovering over a luminous abyss. Then, as the women sit across from each other at the table, Alma rends her bare forearm with her nails and, with an erotically provocative expression, lays it on the table stretched out toward Elisabet. The actress presses her mouth to the wound and bites or sucks it: blood can be seen oozing out under her lips. Whereupon Alma strikes Elisabet's off-screen face furiously and repeatedly. The scene echoes, although with significant differences, the real fight in which Elisabet bloodied Alma's nose. Here vampirism is provoked by the victim, who first seems to enjoy it, then wreaks severe vengeance. What appears to be implied is a symbiotic relationship, but a symbiosis for destruction rather than survival: for mutual rending rather than mutual sustenance.

In the next shot we are back in Elisabet's former hospital room; Alma, in uniform, is tending her docile patient. The nurse talks gently and coaxingly to the actress, persuading her to repeat after her: "Nothing, no nothing." Awkwardly, like someone who hasn't formulated words in a long time, Elisabet repeats: "No-thing." "That's right," says Alma, soothingly, "that's the way it shall be." It would seem that she has broken Elisabet's will, and filled her with a sense of utter futility. So, during a nervous collapse, the poet Theodore Roethke once wrote down this sentence: "The ultimate death is the death of the will." That is what Alma has induced in Mrs. Vogler.

But this, we must remember, is part of that unreal state of nightmare or phantasmagoria recorded by the latter sections of the film, and not meant to be understood as really happening. We see next, faintly and hazily, that first dream of Alma's, in which Elisabet stood behind her and lovingly smoothed back her hair. Then we see Alma waking up with a jump. She is wearing the nightdress she wore in the scene in which Mr. Vogler appeared. We may infer that we have been watching a series of consecutive dreams from that point on, except that Alma wakes up in a markedly different place and position from the ones in which she fell asleep. Dream or not, we can agree with Robin Wood that what we saw was *"in some sense* really happening," and that the women were "really inflicting terrible psychological wounds on each other."

Thereupon sober reality returns. The women are packing their bags without talking to each other; Alma is also storing away terrace furniture inside the cottage. She stops to look at herself in a mirror, and performs her little gesture of smoothing back her hair. In a vision in the mirror, there is Elisabet, again, as in the first dream, smoothing back Alma's hair. Now both women simultaneously stroke Alma's curl off her forehead. The implication seems to be that though they are about to part forever, in Alma's memory (and perhaps in Elisabet's, too) they will remain united.

We see Alma leaving. That mysterious wooden female figurehead, which we have seen earlier in the film (and which, like a mascot, keeps reappearing in Bergman's work—most recently in *The Touch*), is revealed in close-up while, at a distance behind it, Alma is locking the cottage door after her. We do not see Elisabet leave, but immediately after the close-up of the figurehead, there is one of the actress playing Electra again. We note the similarity between the two faces; it may be meant to suggest parallel inscrutabilities behind the surface of the work of art and beneath the persona of the artist. The shot of Mrs. Vogler acting would tend to imply that she is cured and on the stage once more, except that it is the same shot we saw at the beginning of the film and that she is again in front of a camera rather than a theatre audience. We see the camera again, mounted on a platform on a crane, with Bergman and Nykvist sitting behind it. But now comes a new element: there is a shot through the view finder revealing Elisabet supine on a bed, her head hanging over the front edge. We have seen two women in the same position, shot in the same way, before: the old woman in the morgue, and Alma, just before the appearance of Mr. Vogler. In some sense, then, the crone's awakening into life, Alma's setting out on what seems to be a series of dreams or visions, and Elisabet's being photographed in a film within a film correspond to one another. Bergman seems to be saying that life, dream, and art are identical: that being born, having visions, creating a role or some other work of art are basically equivalent activities.

Then we observe Alma catching a bus from the seashore back to town. The camera pans downward and we see the ground covered with a multitude of barren pebbles. From this we go back to the boy of the prologue, again gazing at and reaching for that large, hazy twofold female head that keeps fading in and out on the panel before him. Then, once again, we see the film inside the projector as it comes to the end and runs off the sprockets. Finally, there are the two arc lights sputtering out into THE END. "The subject of *Persona* is the violence of the spirit," writes Susan Sontag. "If the two women violate each other, each can be said to have at least as profoundly violated herself. In the final parallel to this theme, the film itself seems to be violated—to emerge out of and descend back into the chaos of 'cinema' and film-as-object.''

Before we try to interpret *Persona* more thoroughly—and with it the essential characteristics of Bergman's *oeuvre*—we should remind ourselves that the film does not yield entirely to logical explication. As Miss Sontag has rightly pointed out, Bergman has given us not so much a story as "a body of material, a subject," whose function may be precisely "its opacity, its multiplicity." And this certainly includes, as she puts it, "reflections about the nature of representation (the status of the image, of the word, of action, of the film medium itself)." But some possible over-all interpretations of this "multiplicity" need to be broached.

There is, first and most palpably, the relationship of the artist and the worshipful layman. Though Bergman has denied to me the relevance of this interpretation, I must respectfully reject this denial. As Guy Brancourt writes,[*] Bergman's later work is "the expression of the bad conscience of the artist led to meditate on the means and scope of his art as it faces the problems of the world." Or, as I wrote in my original review of *Persona* (reprinted in *Movies into Film* [†]): "The artist and the ordinary human being need each other, but this is a love-hate, a fight for absolute power over the other. Their complete communion is illusory and painful—only a dream, a nightmare—yet also real enough, perhaps, to mark them both. Life and art batten on each other, art sucking life's blood, life trying to cajole or bully art into submission, into becoming its mirror. The result of the strife is madness; whether feigned or real hardly matters. Relatives, lovers, friends, all who are sucked into this conflict, suffer along with the principal combatants. The end is, at best, a draw.''

This interpretation—the conflict between the withdrawn artist and the layman pursuing him with veneration—flows naturally into a related one: the artist caught in an affair with a non-artist. I firmly believe that Bergman is here, at least in part, expiating his treatment of certain women he has been involved with, from whom he took more than he gave, only to end up immersing himself in his work while they were left helpless, fists beating against a locked door. Though the egocentric male lover is disguised here as a woman patient—Bergman is not eager to flaunt intimate autobi-

[*] In this conclusion to the French edition of Jörn Donner's *Ingmar Bergman* (Paris: Seghers, 1970), p. 131.

[†] New York: Dial Press, 1971.

ography—the relationship between Elisabet and Alma has manifestly erotic, passionate characteristics. This is true both of the women's highly emotive hostilities and of the opposite process, their psychic fusion. The heroine of *Hour of the Wolf,* also called Alma, asks her husband, "Isn't it true that old people who have lived together all their lives begin to resemble each other? In the end they have so much in common that not only their thoughts but also their faces take on the same expression." This, certainly, is what happens between the "lovers" Elisabet and Alma; and here, too, Strindberg paved the way for Bergman. In his *Legends,* Strindberg wrote: "We begin to love a woman by depositing with her our souls, bit by bit. We duplicate our personality; and the beloved woman who formerly was indifferent and neutral begins to assume the guise of our other self, becoming our double." Through imaginary identification that ends up producing, whether in love or love-hate, real similarity, one ends up being chained to the woman one loves (and, perhaps, hates) as to one's mirror image, one's double, one's self.

This specific psychosexual conflict is an aspect of a bigger power struggle: the battle of the sexes, as it keeps appearing in Strindberg and, scarcely less frequently, in Bergman. The form it usually takes is humiliation of the adversary, and though this is not always sexual, it most often is. We have already traced the humiliation motif in *The Clown's Evening,* and found it to be equally prominent in *Smiles of a Summer Night,* albeit in a less malign form, as befits a comedy. In *Winter Light,* it is characteristic of Tomas's treatment of Märta, and is echoed, on a social level, by his handling of Frövik, and, on the cosmic level, by God's silence, so profoundly humiliating for a man of Tomas's stamp. In *Persona,* the humiliation of Alma begins with the actress's refusal to respond to the nurse's loving care, intensifies with the letter to the doctor that seems to mock and minimize the nurse, and culminates in the superior laughter with which Elisabet (the male principle in this relationship, even if a passive male wooed by the solicitous female) squelches the nurse's last resort, physical violence. The latter part of the film, then, is a series of reversals, in which Alma, despite minor setbacks, gets the upper hand and humiliates Mrs. Vogler, by making love to her husband in front of her, unmasking her sordid relationship to her son, beating her up, and, finally, both forcing her to speak and obliging her to utter a word of defeat and despair. (That all this is not really "happening" is beside the point.) It is a full spectrum of humiliations, from subtle to ravaging, and it implements Bergman's program, as formulated in the already quoted interview with Sundgren: "I think it's terribly important that art expose humiliation, that art show how human beings humiliate one another, because humiliation is one of the most dreadful companions of humanity, and our whole social system is based to an enormous extent on humiliation. . . ." I am not sure that *Persona* can be stretched to cover humiliations within the social system; but it deals superlatively with sexual and other private humiliations.

It is characteristic, too, that Elisabet Vogler's defiance of life should take the form of silence, which is not only antisocial but also, in a deeper sense, antihuman, and strikes Bergman as particularly sinister. In a number of his films silence is associated with more or less reprehensible doings (the guileful silence of Death in the confessional scene of *The Seventh Seal;* the charlatanic silence of Vogler, Elisabet's namesake in *The Face (The Magician)* the bestial silence of the mute rapist-murderer in *The Virgin Spring;* the eponymous silence of non-communication in Timoka, whose language is a mystery to the main characters of *The Silence;* the silence of God in *Winter Light*). The elected silence of Elisabet is a perfect image of unreachableness; and unhappiness in Bergman—as, I dare say, in life—is generally caused by not being able to grasp someone or something. Silence was the prime tormentor of the lonely child that Bergman once was, in whom, as the preface to *Persona* states, there was an overwhelming need "to get people to listen, to respond, to live in the warmth of a community." And, surely, the child in the morgue sequence of the film, who reappears at the end, is the author with whom it all begins and ends: with a yearning for warmth, for communion with that woman's image, that *Ewig-Weibliche* that twinkles before him, having the dual shape of woman: the cold, brilliant, self-centered glamour of the actress; and the dependable but naïve devotion of the nurse, itself not so pure and simple as might appear.

What makes silence even more culpable than its denial of community, however, is that while it gives nothing, it coaxes or challenges the other person into spilling his most intimate and sacred spiritual possessions. So Miss Y., in *The Stronger,* stole the raw silk from Mrs. X.'s cocoon; so, too, as the image (if not the worm) turned, she burrowed into the healthy fruit of the other woman's existence, eating it all away. For silence is, in the final reckoning, vampirism: a vacuum into which the other person's, the speaker's, lifeblood ebbs as surely as if it were being sucked. By getting Elisabet to suck her blood, Alma is merely making manifest, hideously illustrating, a dire encroachment that was operant from the beginning. Implied, too, must be the dreadful irony of a mouth that will not open to bestow the trifling comfort of speech, but eagerly gapes to take away the other person's vital fluid.

Though it is not wholly inadmissible, the tendency to read *Persona* as the dramatization of a split in a single personality must, finally, be resisted and curtailed. For the merging of opposing tendencies in a single human being is a reconciliation, a blessing; whereas here it is clearly a psychic cataclysm, or, in Brancourt's words, "permeability . . . in the bad sense." It seems clear to me that the film is not, as Pauline Kael glibly claimed, lacking in "a structure of meanings in the work by which an interpretation can be validated." It is, surely, much sounder to say, with Susan Sontag, that "while maintaining the indeterminacy of the situation (from a psychological point of view) Bergman does not give the impression of evading the issue, and presents nothing that is psychologically improbable." It is even more dismaying to read William Pechter's reference to *Persona* as a "muffled mystification," and to read on, as Pechter compounds his folly: "It was Shaw, I believe, who described someone or something as a sphinx without a riddle. A film such as *Persona* seems to me a riddle without a sphinx, an infinitely portentous mystery, lying inert, without the intellect, or art, to make it reverberate." Thus while Miss Kael complains of the unresolvable "expressiveness and fascination of what we are given," Pechter sees only emptiness in the film: "It looks like a volcano. But it is extinct." * How much more just is Wood's estimate that the film "compels us to feel what we are shown with unusual immediacy, as if naked experience were being communicated direct, instead of being clothed with the customary medium of characters-and-narrative."

It is hard, if not impossible, to carry away a message from the film's conclusion. Wood sees *Persona* ending "not with a negation, but with a question mark"; Brancourt perceives "a positive side" in the actress's "return to normal life and the stage . . . even in

---

* William S. Pechter, *Twenty-Four Times a Second* (New York: Harper & Row, 1971). As for that supposedly Shavian epigram, it comes, actually, from Oscar Wilde's *A Woman of No Importance:* "Mrs. Allonby: Define us as a sex. Lord Illingworth: Sphinxes without secrets."

its precariousness, even achieved at the expense of the nurse's equilibrium"; Miss Sontag insists that "mask and person, speech and silence, actor and 'soul' remain divided—however parasitically, even vampiristically, they are shown to be intertwined." I wonder whether the ending, taken Jungianly, is not a nod Bergman grudgingly makes to the *status quo*. As Birgitta Steene writes, "a complete abandonment of our *persona* would, according to Jung, lead to a state of mute unconsciousness; a human being would stand face to face with his naked self (and with the absolute)." But she fails to note the application of this to the film: Elisabet's silence and Alma's facing of the harsh truths about herself prove equally unlivable with. So one woman dons the tragic (or comic) mask again; the other, the nurse's uniform. The need for masks is perhaps dismaying and deplorable (and that may be the reason for the film's running off the sprockets in the end—unless it be that the author's brain simply tires of the struggle of creation, and of the existential battles it has been conveying), but masks do enable life to go on.

At the risk of sounding fanciful, I would like to suggest one further possible interpretation of the film; and it should be noted, by the way, that the various interpretations given do not militate against one another but, rather, provide mutual reinforcement. In a 1969 interview, Bergman said to Peter Cowie: "Film is concerned above all also with *rhythm*. . . . The primary factor is the image, the secondary factor is the sound, the dialogue; and the tension between these two creates the third dimension." It seems to me that one can say that Elisabet's expressions, gestures, reactions create the images of the film, just as Alma's talk creates its sound. And the tension between these two—the absoluteness of the silent image, and the eager relativity of the fragile, corruptible, groping word—creates the superbly three-dimensional film that *Persona* is. For this is the film par excellence in which the processes of the mind are epitomized: the mind creating a film from bits and pieces, the mind defying the world with hostile withdrawal, or being partly coaxed back by affectionate care. And, above all, the mind twisting, hallucinating, snapping in the throes of psychic conflict: *Persona* is as much psychography as cinematography.

Perhaps the self-reflexive nature of the prologue needs to be further explained in this context. For it is not only a recapitulation of previous Bergmaniana; it is also, as I just said, an illustration of

how, from scattered images, a film is born. The cartoon of a woman washing her hands and the filmed image of hands washing, *i.e.,* film as the manifest trickery of the cartoon versus film as the faithful photograph of the real thing (though that, too, is a form of trickery), raises the question of illusion versus reality, particularly as it affects this film. The farce sequence, in which Death and the Devil frighten or pursue a frantic fellow, mirrors the central problem of *Persona:* the actress's trying to retreat from the falseness of (alleged) unreality, and the nurse's attempting to ignore her own reality. It is, also, all of us fleeing from real horrors, like death, or unreal but real-seeming ones, like the Devil. There is no direct connection between the spider in the prologue and the main body of the film, though there is, in the screenplay, a reference to spiders in Elisabet's letter to her doctor, and there is something faintly but undeniably spidery about the way Elisabet leads Alma on. The hand in the entrails of the sheep, followed by a knife heading for the sheep's eye, followed, in turn, by a hand with a nail driven through it seem to stand for the film's (and life's) alternating pattern of victimization and becoming victimized. For, it should be noted, the hand that is being nailed down is held in place by another hand—the victim's own. And the tortured hand is closed at first; only when it opens does the blood flow. The implication seems to be that our wounds are deep and secret; it takes an investigation of the kind *Persona* is to make them bleed openly. The knife about to enter a sheep's eye may be a tribute to Buñuel's *Un Chien andalou,* with its famous eye-gouging scene. If so, it is not a mere arbitrary *hommage,* but the acknowledgment of an important source of *Persona.* In a talk with Marianne Kärré, Bergman remarked: "Have I borrowed anything in *Persona?* But of course. Why wouldn't I borrow? Buñuel was my first cinematic revelation. He remained the most important for me. . . . I entirely share his theory of initial shock to attract the public's attention." *
The assault on the eye, the window of the soul, clearly presages the ruthlessness and pain of the attack on the psyche the film is about to undertake.

The brick wall dissolving into wintry woods suggests getting out of doors after being pent in the hospital, Elisabet and Alma's translation to the seaside. The snowy landscapes and the spiked iron fence are not in the film, but there is something figuratively fenced

* In *Cinéma 66,* Nr. 111, December 1966.

off and snowed in about Elisabet's silence. The dead people awakening may well represent an author's breathing life into his conceptions, and by so doing becoming, like the boy in the prologue, fully alive himself.

I suspect that I have interpreted these liminal images only tentatively, approximately. But I believe that something of the sort is surely implied. It does not matter that these images may also refer to previous Bergman films: that merely demonstrates the consistency, the interrelatedness of his *oeuvre*. What matters is that Bergman has here tipped his hand to us. These, he seems to say, are the images from which I begin; this is how this film—or my other films, or film in general—is born: from these very private, idiosyncratic yet universalizable images.

However universally resonant it may be, though, *Persona,* like *Winter Light,* is a film made to its author's requirements, first and last; there is absolutely no compromising with audience tastes. As Bergman said at the end of his "Snakeskin" speech: "To be an artist for one's own satisfaction is not always so agreeable. But it has one great advantage: the artist coexists with every living creature that lives only for its own sake. Altogether, it makes a pretty large brotherhood existing egoistically on the hot, dirty earth under a cold and empty sky." *Persona* is a shattering statement of despair, but one that, by its very existence and excellence, proves that despair can be sublimated, overcome.

FILMOGRAPHY

THE CLOWN'S EVENING (The Naked Night)
Gycklarnas· Afton   90 minutes
1953

Directed by Ingmar Bergman
Produced by Rune Waldekranz (Sandrews)
Screenplay by Ingmar Bergman
Photographed by Hilding Bladh and Sven Nykvist
Sets by Bibi Lindström
Costumes by Mago
Music by Karl-Birger Blomdahl
Edited by Carl-Olaf Skeppstedt

Cast

Harriet Andersson	Anne
Åke Grönberg	Albert Johansson
Hasse Ekman	Frans
Anders Ek	Frost
Gudrun Brost	Alma
Annika Tretow	Agda
Gunnar Björnstrand	Mr. Sjuberg
Erik Strandmark	Jens
Kiki	The dwarf
Åke Fridell	The officer
Majken Torkeli	Mrs. Ekberg
Vanjek Hedberg	Ekberg's son
Curt Lövgren	Blom

SMILES OF A SUMMER NIGHT

Sommarnattens Leende   110 minutes

1955

Directed by Ingmar Bergman
Production Company: Svensk Filmindustri
Production Manager: Allan Ekelund
Screenplay by Ingmar Bergman
Photographed by Gunnar Fischer
Sets by P. A. Lundgren
Costumes by Mago
Music by Erik Nordgren
Edited by Oscar Rosander
Assistant Director: Lennart Olsson

Cast

Eva Dahlbeck	Desirée Armfeldt
Ulla Jacobsson	Anne Egerman
Harriet Andersson	Petra
Margit Carlquist	Charlotte Malcolm
Gunnar Björnstrand	Fredrik Egerman
Jarl Kulle	Count Carl-Magnus Malcolm
Åke Fridell	Frid
Björn Bjelvenstam	Henrik Egerman
Naima Wifstrand	Madame Armfeldt
Jullan Kindahl	The cook
Gull Natorp	Malla
Birgitta Valberg	Actress
Bibi Andersson	Actress
Anders Wulff	Desirée's son
Gunnar Nielsen	Niklas

Gösta Prüselius, Svea Holst, Hans Straat, Lisa Lundholm,
Sigge Fürst, Lena Söderblom, Mona Malm, Joseph Norman,
John Melin, Sten Gester

WINTER LIGHT

Nattvardsgästerna (The Communicants)   80 minutes

1962

Directed by Ingmar Bergman

314

Production Company: Svensk Filmindustri
Production Manager: Allan Ekelund
Screenplay by Ingmar Bergman
Photographed by Sven Nykvist
Sets by P. A. Lundgren
Edited by Ulla Ryghe
Assistant Director: Lenn Hjortzberg

Cast

Gunnar Björnstrand	Tomas Ericsson
Ingrid Thulin	Märta Lundberg
Max von Sydow	Jonas Persson
Gunnel Lindblom	Karin Persson
Allan Edwall	Algot Frövik
Olof Thunberg	Fredrik Blom
Elsa Ebbeson	Old woman
Kolbjörn Knudsen	Knut Aronsson

PERSONA

1966   81 minutes

Directed by Ingmar Bergman
Production Company: Svensk Filmindustri
Production Manager: Lars-Owe Carlberg
Screenplay by Ingmar Bergman
Photographed by Sven Nykvist
Sets by Bibi Lindström
Costumes by Mago
Music by Lars-Johan Werle
Edited by Ulla Ryghe
Assistant Director: Lenn Hjortzberg

Cast

Bibi Andersson	Alma
Liv Ullmann	Elisabet Vogler
Margaretha Krook	The doctor
Gunnar Björnstrand	Herr Vogler
Jörgen Lindström	The boy